Reflections for the Workplace

Reflections for the Workplace

The Pathway
to a Successful
Job and Career

Bruce N. Hyland
Merle J. Yost

McGraw-Hill
New York   San Francisco   Washington, D.C.   Auckland
Bogotá   Caracas   Lisbon   London   Madrid   Mexico City
Milan   Montreal   New Delhi   San Juan   Singapore
Sydney   Tokyo   Toronto

Library of Congress Cataloging-in-Publication Data

Hyland, Bruce N.
   Reflections for the workplace: the pathway to a successful
job and career / Bruce Hyland, Merle Yost.
      p.   cm.
   ISBN 0-07-031820-4
   1. Vocational guidance. 2. Business etiquette. 3. Business
ethics I. Yost, Merle J. II. Title.
HF5381.H95 1997
650.1—dc21
                                    96-40315
                                        CIP

McGraw-Hill

A Division of The McGraw-Hill Companies

1 2 3 4 5 6 7 8 9 0 DOC/DOC 9 0 2 1 0 9 8 7

ISBN 0-07-031820-4

*The sponsoring editor for this book was Susan Barry, the editing supervisor was
Patricia V. Amoroso, and the production supervisor was Suzanne W. B. Rapcavage.
It was set in Palatino by Terry Leaden of McGraw-Hill's Professional Book Group
composition unit.*

Printed and bound by R. R. Donnelley & Sons Company.

This book is printed on recycled, acid-free paper containing a minimum of 50% recycled, de-inked fiber.

To all of our students, clients, and employees who have taught us to be good managers and better teachers and counselors.

Contents

Working with Others

Conduct

Ethics

Self-Development

The Future

Preface

This is an important book. Not because we say so, but because other people have said so. Many people desperately want and need good career advice. They want advice that "tells it like it is." They want advice that is based in the real world. They want to know the inner secrets of bosses an dwhat it really takes to succeed. This book provides that.

Many people have asked us for career advice over the years and we were only able to give bits and pieces. By writing this, we were able to encapsulate the discoveries and hard lessons we've had to learn personally, along with the shared experiences of other people.

We conducted research with hundreds of people from all types of organizations: Fortune 500 companies, nonprofit and governmental agencies, and small businesses. We've also talked with more people than we could count while we were teaching, training, consulting, and counseling. We found an almost universal truth: People want to be happy in their careers. They want their work to be meaningful. They also want their work environments to be pleasant.

We've also found that most people have never been told how to be successful as an employee. That may be because of a family background where parents weren't able to provide these insights or because someone has immigrated here from another land and another cuture; for whatever reason, this information simply hasn't been available.

We offer this to high school and college counselors who have never had this information to pass on before. The same is true for human resource professionals, career counselors, and organizational trainers. All will benefit from passing this information on to people who need and want it.

We firmly believe that individual employees can make a profound difference in their own working lives. Sure, it helps to have a great boss and to work for a great company, but that's not required. What is required is for employees to follow certain "rules" which have a high probability of making them more successful in working with their boss, with their co-workers, and in their organization as a whole. Quite honestly, if these rules don't work, it's time to seek another position elsewhere.

We don't claim any single rule by itself will produce magic. However, we are absolutely confident that if you apply the majority of these rules in your working life, you will be rewarded personally and profession-ally.

Bruce N. Hyland

Merle J. Yost

Reflections for the Workplace

The Basics

1
HAVE A PROFESSIONAL APPEARANCE

Our professional appearance has an enormous impact on our success. The way we dress, groom, and present ourselves sends a very loud message about how we feel about ourselves…and the less others know us, the more important that message is.

The Trap

There is the *appearance* that organizations don't take this as seriously as in the past. This is an illusion! We think, since there are "casual days," our appearance doesn't matter as much. Or that our appearance has nothing to do with our job performance.

The Professional Role

Our appearance creates our first impression. That impression will help or hurt our career. At first, our appearance is all that is seen. The key is not to distract from your work by having a poor image. Frequently, we don't have or take the time to find out about people, so we make fast assessments. We judge people on their appearance. People who do not care about their appearance are seen as lacking social skills, lacking self-awareness, having low self-esteem, and even having poorer mental health!

We need to dress, groom, and deport ourselves in such a way that we "fit" into the organizational norms of our company. There *is* a social standard; and the higher people go in an organization, the more attention they must pay to their professional appearance.

The Rule at Work

Kerry was hired as an engineer for an international development company. He was exceptionally smart and he had aspirations to move up. The company was a long-established, conservative company.

Kerry arrived for work on the first day dressed in jeans, a sweatshirt, and sunglasses, with a shaved head and two-day beard. His boss seemed a bit distant and disturbed. Kerry couldn't figure out why. This could have been because when Kerry interviewed he had worn his suit and was well groomed—having been coached by the placement counselors at his university. However, since he didn't know what caused his boss's reaction, he assumed first-day jitters and kept on dressing the same way.

Kerry got along with people and worked hard. He received feedback that his work was good. However, he was never invited to give presentations to clients or meet with upper management. He was frustrated since his goal was to get into management.

One day, he asked one of the supervisors whom he trusted to give him some feedback. Kerry asked, "What do you think is going on?" The supervisor counseled, "Kerry, your work is good, but your appearance doesn't fit the image of this company and it certainly doesn't fit for someone who wants to advance. You must 'look' like you fit into the position that you aspire to achieve. Then, people can 'see' you in that position."

Action Steps

Ask a trusted friend to give you a critique of your professional appearance. Throw out the clothing items that really need to be tossed.

Notice the professional appearance of people who hold the type of position you'd like to have someday.

2
DON'T TALK TOO MUCH; LET OTHERS TALK

If we're talking, we're not listening. Listening brings information, knowledge, and power. In some cases, the more we talk, the more it shows how little we know.

The Trap

We all know people who talk too much and who never listen. They have fallen into the trap of assuming that everyone is interested in what they are saying. Or they are talking a lot to cover their insecurity or nervousness. Unfortunately, that's obvious to everyone except the person who is overtalking.

The Professional Role

When we make our point and then stop talking and listen, we are signaling that we are interested and open to hearing other people. That usually prompts the others into sharing their information or point of view. Through this exchange, we can expand our horizons and communicate.

When we find the right balance between talking and listening, we are showing courtesy and respect. How do we find that balance? We make our point. We're succinct and get to the core of what we want to communicate. If the other people want more, they will ask. By doing this, we may avoid an embarrassing faux pas. Once we get the reputation of being talkers, people start avoiding us and making some very unflattering comments about us when we can't hear them.

The Rule at Work

Teresa was a real estate appraiser for a mortgage lender. She saw herself as a "people person" and loved to talk with people. So far, so good. However, early in her career she overdid it a bit and it got her into trouble.

When she first started in this job, she was naturally nervous. Since she was a social person, she compensated by talking—too much. She wouldn't get to the point. She would chatter on and on. In doing so, she would take up her coworkers' time, which they began to resent.

Teresa had the biggest problem in meetings and presentations given by the company's management. Again, in order to impress her superiors, she always spoke out and went on and on about her ideas and opinions. While the management valued input, there was an appropriate level of input and conversation. Teresa repeatedly violated that.

That was early in her career, however. Someone must have advised her about her overtalking, because all of a sudden she started listening more. She asked questions. She still made her points, but then she shut up and listened. When being social, she paid attention to the other person and encouraged him or her to talk as much, if not more, than she did. She's quite successful now. She's respected and has lots of friends.

Action Steps

Monitor your talking. See how much you talk and how much you listen. Keep it in balance.

The next time you're telling someone something, get to the point and then be quiet. See if the other person asks for more.

If you're prone to nervous chatter, start timing yourself. Don't go on for more than a minute or two.

3
BE TACTFUL

Tact is knowing what to say (or not say) and when to say it (or not say it). Without sacrificing the message or the truth, deliver your message in such a way that it honors the humanity of the other person involved.

The Trap

All of us want to communicate with people. The trap is that even though the information is important, delivering it at a time or in a way that it cannot be heard will result in the message not being received and possibly the messenger being punished.

The Professional Role

Astute professional employees will realize that they need to communicate some things and not communicate others. They also realize that timing, the situation, and appropriateness are keys to people being able and willing to hear what they have to say. That's tact. It is possible to say anything if it is said correctly.

Certainly, we all have information which we need to share with others, individually or as a group. A successful person, however, will realize that an important message needs to be delivered in such a way that other people can benefit from the message.

Tactful people are respected people, and they are usually very effective because their messages get heard.

The Rule at Work

Rob was getting ready to retire. The people who were arranging his retirement party went around asking coworkers about Rob in order to use that information in their acknowledgment of him.

One of the main things that his colleagues said about Rob was that he was tactful. "Well, what does that mean?" asked the event organizers.

"Over the years, Rob has told me lots of good things and also given me some helpful feedback that wasn't necessarily fun to hear," one fellow employee said. "He was sensitive enough to know when I was up to hearing the negative feedback and also lavished his praise to balance it out. He understands the importance of timing. That's tact!"

Another colleague said, "Rob knew when to keep his mouth shut. He knew a lot about each of us…some very personal things. Even when others might be teasing us or bringing up stuff we didn't want mentioned, Rob would just sit silently. He knew how to be appropriate. That's tact."

His boss said, "One time I was delivering a presentation and my pants zipper was unzipped. As I was walking up to the podium Rob noticed and instead of yelling out, 'Paul, your fly's undone!' he dropped something intentionally so that it caught my attention and then signaled me. That's tact."

At his retirement luncheon, Rob's coworkers were tactful enough not to remind him of the time he dyed his hair to try to look younger.

Action Steps

Think of someone who is very tactful. What is one thing that person does which you admire?

Determine one upcoming situation where you will need to use some tact.

Identify the type of situation in which it is most difficult for you to be tactful.

4
HAVE RESPECT FOR OTHERS

By giving respect to others, you receive it in return. In effect, this is the Golden Rule in action...and it works in organizations just as well as in life.

The Trap

The bottom line to this trap is believing that we're superior in some way. "So what if she thinks of me that way." Maybe they aren't as educated, as popular, or as attractive. Or maybe they are a different race, religion, or culture. "I'm better" is the thought. "You're not as good as me" is the message.

The Professional Role

When we show respect for others, we are treated with respect. We enjoy the good feelings that result from being on equal ground. We feel like "adults" and good human beings. In addition, we enjoy the benefits and fun of a harmonious working environment.

Having respect for others can be as simple as showing common courtesies: a good morning greeting, holding the door to let someone pass, waiting in line courteously, or waiting our turn to speak up at a meeting.

Having respect for others can also be quite complicated and difficult (if we have feelings of intolerance). Respect may mean examining and wrestling with our feelings, and learning some new ways of interacting with people around issues of gender, race, culture, age, sexual orientation, religion, or physical limitation.

The Rule at Work

Tom sold insurance for a company in the Midwest. He was middle-aged, had worked for the company over 15 years, and was very set in his ways and opinions. Those opinions were not always very respectful of people.

He barked at some of his colleagues when he was having a bad sales week. He would interrupt people in meetings or even in his sales presentations with clients. He made jokes about minority groups and found something wrong with everyone—except himself.

Why did the company keep him on? He made enough sales to hold on, and he didn't have a particularly strong manager. Then, like most of us, he hit some rough waters in his life. First, his sales were poor for the first half of the year. Then, in an argument with one of his coworkers, he made some racist remarks and was slapped with a lawsuit. When the hard times came, he didn't have anyone there supporting him. He felt isolated and besieged. Then Tom had a heart attack.

As with many people who experience significant life-changing events, Tom emerged from his recuperation with a different view on life. He softened. He saw other people in a different light. He started interacting with everyone differently. He actually became a defender of people who were being put down by others. In sum, Tom developed a lot of respect for others.

Action Step

Choose one of your habits that could be interpreted as disrespectful and change it.

Do a self-assessment. Do you feel superior to others? How does it show up?

Ask for feedback from a good and trusted friend. Ask that person how you could show more respect for others.

5
KNOW THE RULES OF ETIQUETTE

What you don't know will *hurt you. There are various protocols that are appropriate for different situations. Your manners (etiquette) are visible and judged by all around you.*

The Trap

In today's relaxed working environment, it's easy to believe that manners, protocol, and etiquette really don't matter. Not true.

Perhaps we were not trained in how to conduct ourselves in professional social situations, but just as in the law, not knowing is not an excuse.

The Professional Role

We don't have to be Ms. Manners to know and use the rules of etiquette, manners, and protocol. We simply need to know the basics of what's to be done and how to do it in various professional and social situations. Doing so will set us apart and open doors for careers.

To be successful, we need to understand and practice the conventionally accepted ways of acting in society.

Most of us want to do the right things, to be accepted socially and professionally. Fortunately, there are many ways to learn these "rules." There are books we can read and people that we can ask for coaching and guidance; or we can watch people whom we respect, see what they do, and copy them.

The Rule at Work

Faris was a bank teller. He was hardworking and wanted to progress within the bank. He was American but born outside the United States. He was proud of the fact that he had learned many of the social and professional customs required to be successful in business.

He had learned how to meet and greet people, how to engage them in small talk in order to establish rapport (this was not the custom in his country), how to attend a formal business dinner, when to arrive (which was *really* different from his country), and how to properly address various important people.

He was always amazed, however, when some new aspect of etiquette surfaced. During one particular week he faced a difficult situation. He was invited to attend an "employee's session with the vice president." He thought that meant that he was to tell the vice president all the things that he thought were wrong with the bank. His friend counseled him, "Some real input might be valued, but don't overdo it. They will be watching you to see if you can create positive relationships with others."

Faris kept watching what other successful employees did. He asked when he didn't know. He even purchased a book on business etiquette. To his delight, many of his American friends eventually came to him for advice on the proper way to do things.

Action Steps

Thumb through a book on business etiquette. If there are things in there that are unfamiliar, buy it.

Help one of your colleagues by gently and privately mentioning one aspect of etiquette that is getting in the way of his or her career progress.

Learn about the customs of your coworkers from other cultures.

6
UNDERSTAND THE CHAIN OF COMMAND

Be aware of both the formal and informal chain of command. Use it as a road map to get things done, reach your goals, and avoid problems.

The Trap

The main trap is believing that the chain of command does not apply to us. Going around or over a boss is a power play for which we may have to pay the price. Not understanding how decisions are made and who really makes them will prevent us from succeeding. We shouldn't let frustration interfere with our better judgment.

The Professional Role

The formal chain of command is the organization chart that we see on the wall...showing who answers to whom. It is the decision-making path. The rule of the formal chain is to go up only one level to your boss with ideas, questions, etc. and let him or her carry them upward.

The informal chain of command is different. This refers to the people who truly *influence* the decision making, yet who might not be on the chart or who might be in positions which do not *appear* to have much authority. The informal chain of command is usually as strong as, if not stronger than, the formal one. The rule for the informal chain is to use it with great discretion and sensitivity.

We simply need to be aware of both chains in order to accomplish our goals.

The Rule at Work

Jeff was an auditor for a state agency. He likes to tell this story about himself: "I'm a guy who believes in following the rules. But, being human, early in my career I found myself doing the exact opposite. I wanted decisions made faster so I would `go around' my boss to his boss. Man, did I get blasted for that! It didn't take me too many times to realize that that was simply unacceptable at this agency. Sure, I could be friendly and talk with more senior people, but I was expected to take organizational issues to my boss, who was then responsible to take them to his boss, and so on. Now I can see how funny it is that I am so rule-oriented, and yet I was breaking one of the rules."

Jeff's story continues: "The real eye-opener for me, however, was in recognizing the informal chain of command. I wondered why some people seemed to have enormous influence while not holding a corresponding position on the organizational chart. I also wondered why successful employees would go to these people in addition to following the formal chain. Now I know! One day I needed to have an exception made to a procedure. My boss and my boss's boss were gone, so I went to Mary, a senior colleague who was not a manager, but who seemed to have a lot of influence. She quietly told me that she'd see what she could do. Minutes later I got a call from a senior manager who told me to go ahead with the exception."

Action Steps

If you've not reviewed the formal organization chart lately, get a copy today.

Identify three people in your company who have influence way beyond the level of their formal position.

What does this tell you about position, relationship, and power?

7
SHOW RESPECT FOR AUTHORITY

We all have to answer to other people. By the nature of their authority, position, and power, we need to show respect to these people.

The Trap

This is a dangerous area loaded with pitfalls. Beware! Since some of us have experienced bad bosses, we may believe that those in authority don't deserve respect. Or the trap occurs if we don't accept the idea that there are different levels within an organization which require different levels of deference.

The Professional Role

The vast majority of people in authority have earned their positions. They have access to more information and thus see a bigger picture, which we often do not. Because they have earned it in some way, and because they are human, we owe them some respect. We need to show that. Put yourself in their shoes: How would you want to be treated?

The respect we speak of is paying attention, listening, waiting if someone is a few minutes late, adhering to the accepted company protocol about how to interact with others, etc. This may be critically important when doing business with people from other cultures.

If you are unsure, follow the lead of successful coworkers you respect as they interact with authority.

The Rule at Work

Laura was a stockbroker for a major brokerage house. She had been with the firm for about a year and had achieved a better-than-average degree of success. As such, she was being noticed by the firm's management because they thought that she had potential.

Some of her success was due to the fact that Laura was assertive and bold. Her strength was also her weakness. When she was invited to meetings and events with people in authority, she would drop the accepted protocol of calling them Mr. or Ms. X until invited to call them by their first name. Laura just went ahead on a first-name basis, ignoring that small sign of respect. She also criticized management when they were late.

One day when several important clients were visiting, she committed a corporate sin by failing to show respect to the people with authority. Instead of being more formal (as was the custom at this office) when she addressed the visitors and management, she was very informal; she disagreed with the vice president in front of the visitors; and when she heard them hint that she should listen to the presentation, she said that she had heard it before and would return when it was finished.

Laura was finished at this firm. Here was a bright person with potential for a great career, but her inability to recognize the importance of showing respect or her unwillingness to do so was her undoing.

Action Steps

Notice how the successful people at your level show respect for authority in your company.

Identify someone in authority that you need to show more respect for.

When you're in more formal situations, pay special attention to showing respect for authority.

Attitude

8
HAVE PATIENCE

Patience is a virtue. Like most virtues, however, having it isn't always easy. Yet, there can be great rewards.

The Trap

We fear not getting what we want. We don't trust that things will work out naturally. We try to "force" them. We try to make people and situations give us what we want when we want it.

The Professional Role

Patience means quiet waiting. It takes a mature frame of mind to have patience. It's not always fun. In fact, it can be very exasperating. Yet, it is worth the struggle. Whether it's in learning something new, shepherding a project, working towards a promotion, or dealing with a coworker, patience pays off.

There is a close tie between patience and tolerance. And there is a big difference. When we tolerate something, we are willing to wait—but usually for only a short time. On the other hand, when we're patient, we are willing to wait for a long time. When we're patient, we frequently must be open-ended about the outcome. That is, we must wait until the event, project, issue, or whatever takes its natural course.

We learn to trust that things sometimes turn out better than we expected simply because we have patience.

The Rule at Work

Jennifer was a dental technician. She had just graduated from school and was eager to become a success in her career. By nature, she was eager and assertive. Jennifer knew that it was important for the dentists in this practice not only to serve patients well, but also to get them in and out as quickly as possible. So, she set out to get everything done quickly.

However, her impatience was starting to be problematic in other areas. After a month, she told the administrator that she wanted a raise. When the administrator told her that reviews are done every six months, Jennifer became moody for the rest of the day. When the dentists had a staff meeting and said that they were thinking of adding an employee retirement plan "sometime next year," Jennifer started pushing them to get it done this year.

Finally, a friend asked her to coffee and said, "Jennifer, you're a great employee, but your impatience is getting out of hand. Granted we all need to work quickly and efficiently, but some things just take time. You're pushing it; and not only are you annoying people, but also you're showing your immaturity. Please continue to be the committed and caring person you are, but develop some patience—for others, for the tasks, and most importantly, for yourself."

Action Steps

Identify a project or task that you've been trying to "force." For a while, wait quietly for an opportunity to influence it.

Ask three respected colleagues how patience has paid off for them.

Write a "Patience Contract" with yourself: "I will be patient with [X or Y or Z]. By doing so, I expect these payoffs: [list anticipated results]."

9
DEVELOP A CAN-DO ATTITUDE

The first step is believing that you can do it. Develop the self-confidence to try. It's the assumption of success that provides the spark.

The Trap

Many of us share the feeling that we may not be up to the task. It's that fear of failure and the fear of looking like we don't know what we're doing that stops us. We get trapped in our lack of self-confidence.

Some of us also have a fear of looking foolish, so we don't even try. Clearly, we've found another trap here. We only see and communicate why we can't do something or why something won't work. So, we end up not even trying.

The Professional Role

Successful people are willing to try. They don't let their self-doubts stop them. They are positive and upbeat about their abilities. They have an aura of willingness. They assume that they can do things, even if they haven't done this exact thing before.

They focus on their past successes and have learned from their failures. They have that can-do attitude. They believe that they have been prepared to do the task. They realize that other people have confidence in them also.

While they may temporarily hesitate, they are willing to "fake it until they make it." They embrace the project or goal and say to themselves, "I don't know exactly how, but I know I can do it—somehow."

They focus on the "somehow" part. They are willing to try many ways, knowing that they will eventually find a way to succeed.

The Rule at Work

Angela was a sales representative for a pharmaceutical company. When she was hired by this company, she had never been in sales before. She was a little scared, but she was determined to succeed.

Angela was given her territory. She was sent to sales training classes. Then she was told to "go sell." Angela quickly found out that this was the "real world" she'd heard about. It was tough, and she met with temporary setbacks. However, she had a can-do attitude.

She was willing to keep trying and trying and trying. She knew she could do it, even if she didn't exactly know how. Because she wasn't locked into a certain way of selling, she discovered things that really worked. She learned from her mistakes. She knew in her heart that she could do this.

That can-do attitude paid off. Angela became district manager after only two years and is now the divisional sales manager.

Action Steps

Tackle something that you have been hesitant to do. You'll surprise yourself.

Make a list of past successes, including little ones. That's your foundation.

Give yourself a pep talk twice a day. Tell yourself that you can do it.

10
DON'T WORRY IF PEOPLE AREN'T WORKING
AS HARD AS YOU ARE

Set your own working standards. Do not let other people drag your perform-ance down. In the long run, your efforts will be noticed.

The Trap

When we see some people who do not seem to do "their fair share," it is tempting to do just enough to get by—to do no more than they do. The problem is that there is often a long lag time between behavior and reward, and it appears that there are no consequences. Some peo-ple *do* get by with working less than others. They *do not* pull their share of the load. Sooner or later, though, it does get noticed.

The Professional Role

Great employees see beyond the trap and realize that there will be some long-term payoffs to giving a fair day's work for a day's pay. To them, it is as much a matter of integrity as it is a strategic career move.

Professionals make a bargain and honor it. They agree to give the employer their full commitment while at work, completing the tasks assigned.

Like any good businessperson, they realize that if they honor their bargain—a day's work for a day's pay—they will be considered when another opportunity arises. If they don't honor the bargain, they are seldom asked to explore other possibilities.

The Rule at Work

Paul noticed that some people really gave the job "their all" and that others were just there to get the paycheck. He began thinking that the people in the same jobs got paid about the same whether they were real "company people" or they just "showed up." Understandably, he was tempted to just show up and get by with as little as necessary to keep his job and devote his real energy to having fun after work.

"Hey, Paul, don't go out of your way," advised Jerry, a "seasoned" employee of the company who did the least amount of work possible in order to maintain his job. "Heck, look at me. Nothing ever happens to me and I am certainly not a company man."

Paul talked with other employees who were seen more as team players, who were respected by colleagues and management alike, and who were enthusiastic about their work and the contribution they were making to the organization. He felt that there was something unique and special about them. They had the integrity to give full value, to work hard, for their paycheck.

Paul concentrated on giving a full and committed day's work for his day's pay. He felt good about helping his colleagues meet the goals and serve the purpose of the company. He felt good about himself. He respected himself, and others respected him as well.

Action Steps

How much time do you spend comparing and despairing about others?

Pretend you own the company and look honestly at yourself (as an employee). Are you earning your paycheck?

Who is the employee you respect most in the organization? What do you need to do to give yourself that same respect?

11
YOU ARE RESPONSIBLE FOR YOUR FEELINGS AND ACTIONS

Ultimately, you are responsible for your feelings and how you choose to respond to them. Don't let them overwhelm you. Know what you ultimately want before you act.

The Trap

Being unable to control our feelings is the ultimate trap. We believe that we're at the mercy of our feelings. (Not true.) Somehow we view feelings as things that are inflicted upon us instead of coming from inside us.

The Professional Role

Thoughts precede feelings. Feelings precede actions. Thus, our thoughts set us into motion. It's how we interpret our feelings that determines what actions are set into place.

We all have feelings. That's human and healthy. It's what we do with our feelings that matters. The important point is not to get lost in our feelings but to remember the bigger picture. That's not to deny that we can't justify our feelings and actions, but that doesn't mean that it's the best thing to do or in our best interests.

How we act on our feelings is truly about us, not about the other person or about the event that precipitated it. The way we handle our feelings speaks volumes about who we are, our attitude, our self-esteem, our self-control, and our professionalism.

We must be willing to step outside our own worldview. Perhaps we need to see a situation from the other person's point of view. After all, nobody will ever see it exactly the way you do. Then, we need to realize that we're truly in charge of our feelings and actions.

The Rule at Work

Dan was a bus driver for the local transit authority. He had a hot temper, which had gotten him into trouble previously. It was well known that any little thing might send him into a rage and then he'd stomp into management's office, report it, demand action, and stir up trouble.

One day, Dan felt a pain in his chest. Then he blacked out. Later he awoke in a hospital bed. He was lucky. He had survived a heart attack. Something profound happened along with that heart attack. Dan started to realize that his emotions were killing him. Having come back from the edge of death, he also had a much larger perspective about what was important and what wasn't.

He was a changed man. He still had feelings and he still got angry. However, he could step back and ask himself, "Is this worth dying for? What's really important here? What would be a healthy and responsible action?" To everyone's amazement, including his own, he started being more responsible for his feelings and actions.

He talked with the other drivers who had trouble dealing with their feelings and actions. He told them, "Hey, you don't have to have a heart attack to get the lesson I got. You have control over your emotions. *You* are responsible for how you feel about things and the actions you take."

Action Steps

When your feelings start overwhelming you, take a time-out.
Ask a friend for feedback on how you handle your feelings and actions.
If you're stressed, find a safe and appropriate way to express your feelings.

12

THINGS WON'T ALWAYS TURN OUT THE WAY YOU WANT

There are no guarantees. The only aspect you can really control is you. You can influence people and outcomes, but ultimately you cannot control them.

The Trap

We love to believe that we are in complete control of people and events. We like to think that we know how others will react and respond. We also fall prey to assuming that everyone wants the same outcome as we do. We just trust that things will always work the way we want.

The Professional Role

Sometimes things will turn out better than we expect. Sometimes things will turn out worse than we expect. That's just life. It's only an illusion that we can control everyone and everything in our lives.

It's important to be hopeful and to have a positive outlook. That influences the outcomes. Yet, there are so many variables in any situation, that there are bound to be surprises, despite our best efforts to eliminate them. The antidote is to temper our enthusiasm and expectations with a dose of reality.

We simply must not tie our self-image and our self-worth into a pre-defined outcome. We work towards things. We influence them. But we don't control them. Events change. People change. Goals change. We must not let the stress of juggling all those changes get us down.

In fact, many things turn out better than we ever expected. Often, short-term disappointments turn into long-term successes.

The Rule at Work

Halina was an actress. While not internationally famous, she made a good living in her profession. The actors for a large theater troupe asked her to spend a morning giving them advice on their careers.

With the 46 actors seated all around her, she began, "I know that being an actor is a tough life. You've all crossed the first hurdle, and you all have jobs with this troupe. That's your foundation for success."

She continued, "This profession, like all professions, will have many twists and turns. You'll face disappointments. Things won't always turn out the way you want them to. At other times, you'll be astounded at your good luck when events unfold infinitely better than you expected. The best you can do is your best. Keep moving toward your goals, but don't become so stuck on them that you break when something happens to throw them temporarily off course."

Halina mused, "I remember when I was starting out. I wanted to be a great star. I'm now 57 years old and I'm not a great star, but I am a respected actor and I make a good living at it. I still hold that dream, but so far, it hasn't turned out that way. Yet, being on the path is great fun.

"I came to the conclusion that I had to be responsible for working toward my goals, but that I also had to be flexible enough to handle whatever happened as the course of events unfolded."

Action Steps

Ask yourself, "What am I still upset about that didn't go my way?"
Write down the lessons you learned from those experiences.
Give yourself a mourning period to be upset about them, then move forward.

13

SEE THE POSITIVE SIDE OF CONFLICT

Conflict brings clarity. It gives us the chance to reach a new consensus. It is an opportunity if we're willing to see it that way.

The Trap

Many people fear conflict. It's that fear that traps people. We avoid conflict at all costs. We run away, seeing conflict only as negative. We can also get lost in the conflict—forgetting the big picture, forgetting that it's just a single issue instead of the world crashing in on us.

The Professional Role

The opportunity in conflict is to redefine the issue, or the relationship with a coworker or boss, in a better way. Conflict brings clarity. It forces us to consider different perspectives, different visions of how things should be, and different methods of doing things.

As a result we can work toward unifying our ways of accomplishing tasks, our views of a situation, or our expectations for the future. If we do that, conflict is very positive. The key is to be *willing* to look at it from another person's perspective. To do that, we need to check our ego and discuss the disagreement openly, rationally, and with an intention of finding a mutually acceptable resolution.

An interesting and valuable perspective is to keep in mind that people who get into conflict actually care. They care about what is going on. They care about the relationship with the other person. They care about making the situation turn out. It may be hard to accept that in the heat of conflict, but it's true.

The Rule at Work

Natalee was the receptionist at a large law firm. She had a very pleasant personality, and she didn't like conflict. Curiously enough, she found herself around people who seemed to thrive on conflict. In fact, their careers were about conflict.

Natalee tried to avoid disagreements at first. There were the expected disagreements with high-ego lawyers. However, there were also the disagreements with other staff workers and the occasional disagreement with her boss. Natalee would go home at night and find herself worrying about the conflict.

Finally, she couldn't stand it any longer. She took a leap of faith and spoke her mind. To her surprise, the other people listened. They still didn't always agree, but then they were able to talk about it from both sides. Even though it was tough at first, she felt a lot better when she was able to see the positive side of conflict.

Eventually, she got to the point where she accepted conflict as natural. She learned that a simple conflict could bring about good things: clarity, better decisions, and stronger working relationships.

Action Steps

Vow to face the one conflict you've been avoiding. Do it this week.

For that conflict, identify valid perspectives from both sides.

Before you begin, think of the bigger picture: the importance of good working relationships, a successful outcome, or clarity about the future.

14
CARE ABOUT THE SUCCESS OF THE BUSINESS

Invest some energy and emotion into the success of your organization. Care about it. Show that. Doing so will move you and the business forward.

The Trap

Many employees develop the attitude of "It's just a job. Why should I care?" We only invest enough energy to hold on to our jobs and get our paychecks. We resist the investment of ourselves into the organization. Then we wonder why we feel so victimized by our jobs.

The Professional Role

If a business is successful, there are more opportunities for career development, promotions, and raises. A business that struggles or fails offers little or no hope of a career going anywhere. That's the opportunity that sharp employees see. If for no other reason than to keep our jobs, we need to invest some of ourselves into the success of the organization.

Show you care. Take action and let people know that you're investing yourself in the success of this enterprise. Focus on the company's goals and help reach them. This will set you apart and may provide handsome dividends. Even if it doesn't result in direct financial rewards, you will have a greater pride in yourself and what you are doing. When you're trying to make a difference, work has more meaning, is more interesting, and becomes more fun.

The Rule at Work

Kevin was an export clerk with an international shipping company. It was a big company and Kevin was one of what seemed like many export clerks. He didn't much care for his work, but it was a job. He also didn't much care about the success of the business as long as he got his paycheck.

Along came more companies that were starting shipping operations and then came an economic downturn. Kevin's company lost money for three straight quarters. Rumors began flying around the company about layoffs. Suddenly, Kevin became very concerned about the success of the business because his paycheck was now, in fact, threatened.

He, along with hundreds of other employees, began working very hard (and smart) in order to get the company through the troubled times. They succeeded. Then, many of the employees fell back into their old patterns.

Not Kevin. He saw how important it was to care about the company's success. He kept working with that attitude, and his actions reflected that. He got bigger raises than his coworkers and, when we last heard from him, was being considered for the management training program.

Action Steps

How would your work be different if you cared about the success of the business?

Do something this week which makes you feel like you made a real contribution to the organization's success.

Notice the employees throughout your organization. Who cares? Who doesn't? Who would you want working for you?

15

BE LOYAL

Loyalty creates great respect. It builds a solid relationship. It makes you feel better about the organization and the people who work there.

The Trap

People who have fallen into this trap are easy to spot. They walk around and behave with the attitude, "I don't owe this company anything. I'm just paid to be here, not to like them. Anyway, they're not loyal to me, why should I be loyal to them?"

The Professional Role

Loyalty is respecting the confidences and image of your boss and organization. You should be a promoter and defender of the company, speaking positively, even when there are some negatives. Loyalty is also the willingness to "stick it out" through the rougher times, remembering and valuing the good things about the boss and organization more than any temporary troubles. As long as you work for an organization, you're actually paid for a certain degree of loyalty.

You see layoffs and downsizing, and it is harder to be loyal when it appears that companies are less than loyal to their employees. It may even feel like an unequal equation to offer your loyalty if you don't see it returned. However, you need to look at the bigger picture and ask the question, "In general, is my company doing me more good than bad?" If the answer is yes, then you owe some loyalty.

The Rule at Work

Lisa was a real estate salesperson in a 29-person agency. She was a successful agent who had been with the company over 11 years. While 11 years is not a great length of time, Lisa found herself being one of the "old-timers" at this agency. She wondered why.

One day she was waiting for her client and she was pondering that question. "I guess it comes down to loyalty," she thought. "It seems like many people jump ship when they hit the rough water. They run to the next agency, bad-mouthing this one in order to make themselves look smart for leaving. Usually, they find the same things happen over there as they found here. The industry is sort of like that."

She continued to think, "For the most part, my sales manager has been good to me. She isn't perfect, but who is? And for the most part, this agency has been good to me. It isn't perfect, but I don't think there is a perfect company. I made some mistakes, and they stuck by me. They've made some mistakes, so I've stuck by them."

There were undoubtedly times when Lisa didn't get her way and was unhappy, and when she disagreed with management. Still, she didn't go out in the public and criticize them or try to destroy their image. Instead she promoted and defended the agency.

Action Steps

What does loyalty mean to you in your work situation? Does it show?

Do something to demonstrate your loyalty to the company this week.

Think of your relationships at work. To whom are you loyal, and who is loyal to you?

16
BE A TEAM PLAYER

Your actions affect others. Their actions affect you. Work together and go in the same direction.

The Trap

One attitude which gets us into trouble is believing that our way is the only way—that "their" way is wrong, or too slow, or not progressive enough, or that it takes too much effort to work with them. Sometimes we are even more selfish. We believe that we can't shine if we are part of a group.

The Professional Role

While we may act individually, we must think organizationally. That is, we must be team players. We must work with others to achieve the organizational goals. This is not always easy, but it always pays off in the long run.

Being team members requires us to work together, to polish our social skills. It requires compromise and negotiation. Most of all it requires an awareness of others around us, their feelings, and their perspectives. In fact, one of the most powerful social skills team members develop is the willingness and ability to see something from another person's perspective. This allows us to create the magic that a team can produce.

It's like a dance. Sometimes we lead and sometimes we follow. It's easier that way. The whole load is not on our shoulders or on any one person's shoulders. Being team members takes less energy and makes the work more fun.

The Rule at Work

Carmela was a paralegal in a large law firm. There were 72 lawyers, 18 paralegals, and 21 secretaries. Because she was assigned to various projects, Carmela was constantly working with different teams. She noticed that sometimes things went very well, and at other times, things were pretty lousy.

She thought about it and came to the conclusion that people saw themselves more as individual contributors than as part of a team. In fact, some people didn't even like using the word *team*.

Carmela knew that she couldn't change everyone, so she made a wise decision. She would do everything *she* could to be a team player. She consulted with people before she went off in any particular direction in order to see if they had any input or if it would affect them. She asked for help when she needed it; shared and sought helpful information; asked people about their work so she could understand how it impacted her and the organization. She pulled her own weight and helped other people out when they temporarily couldn't handle all of their load (and received help back when she found she actually needed it a time or two). In other words, she became a team player.

Eventually, a few others started acting the same way. Not everyone joined in; but overall it was a much better place to work, and the productivity skyrocketed.

Action Steps

Do one thing today which really demonstrates that you are a team player.

Ask your teammates or colleagues what information they think would be valuable for you to know about their projects.

This week, offer to help someone who could use a little extra help.

17
ACCEPT CHANGE

Flow with change or be crushed by it. Why? Change is inevitable. Develop the flexibility to adapt to and, in some cases, enjoy change.

The Trap

First, there is the trap of assuming that what is true and solid today will be true and solid tomorrow. That is the trap of denial. The second trap is the opposite, catching those who love change. It's the pitfall of changing just for the sake of changing. It creates chaos and wastes energy and other valuable resources.

The Professional Role

Smart employees understand that change is a constant. One of the keys to success is finding a successful way of dealing with change. We can either grow and move forward or stay the same and be left behind.

We meet this exciting challenge by creating in ourselves a way of viewing the workplace (and life) that allows for change and even embraces it when we see its advantages. By doing so, we become comfortable with change. We realize that safety and security actually come from inside us rather than from an outside "guarantee."

We need to pay attention to what's changing at work, in our industry, in the economy, in the country, and in the world. We must notice what new skills are being sought and what abilities are being valued in the new employees. Finally, we should search out the technological changes going on around us and see how they will impact us and our future.

The Rule at Work

Jason was a marketing assistant for an agricultural products wholesaler. About the time he was celebrating his 40th birthday and his 20th anniversary with the company, he began to feel uneasy about his job.

He made note of several factors which contributed to his anxiety. The company had not had any layoffs, although competitors had. New employees at this company were required to have significant computer skills, and he barely knew how to start the computer on his desk. When he read the classified ads, he noticed that marketing assistant jobs were now requiring a background in statistical analysis and many positions were requiring some knowledge of international marketing. To add to this, Jason knew for a fact that the whole agricultural industry had changed dramatically over the past 20 years.

Jason decided to "jump aboard the change wagon" to see where it would take him. He enrolled in a computer course. He planned to take an international marketing course and statistics course once he finished the computer studies. He decided to talk at length with at least one knowledgeable person in the agricultural products industry each month to learn what changes they thought were coming.

After a while he found that he had grown both as a person and in his ability to do his job. He also knew that he had made himself a much more valuable employee. Most of all, Jason found that he actually enjoyed this new way of embracing change.

Action Steps

Identify three changes that are occurring within your organization.
Identify three changes that are occurring within your industry.
Write one personal action plan for each of these changes.

18
BE FLEXIBLE

Work life is filled with give-and-take. Flexibility gives you the ability to stand up to the winds of changing demands and priorities. Rigidity will cause you to break.

The Trap

We often trap ourselves into believing that our way is the only way or that our way is the "right" way. To some, being accommodating means surrendering. To others, letting go of their views is a fate worse than death. We develop a vested interest in our position. Our egos get tied into the process, resulting in our feeling victimized and isolated.

The flip side to this is people who are too flexible. They are not able to contribute anything because they have no position.

The Professional Role

Priorities and work demands are constantly changing. Therefore, we must be flexible. Being in an organization is about give-and-take and finding a balance between your opinion and the opinions of others.

Flexibility is accepting other possibilities, including the possibility that another way may actually be better than our way. Frequently, this happens when we get more information. It is information that allows us to understand and see things from different viewpoints. Thus, we are supported in our flexibility because we see the advantages.

Flexibility is also the willingness to have and to state an opinion (when appropriate) and to let that opinion go when it is not embraced by our boss or our coworkers. This is about give-and-take and going with the flow. It makes work much easier.

The Rule at Work

Otis was one of six printers working in the corporate headquarters of a major company. He was good at his work, but Otis had strong opinions about everything. In and of itself, that was not a problem, but once he formed an opinion he was absolutely rigid about it. There was no room for alternate opinions or other ways of doing things.

When his performance review time came around, he was criticized for his inflexibility in working with people. He was quite surprised by this comment and began defending why he wasn't rigid. "This is just the point," his manager began. "You need to search for the thought and possible truth in other people's views." The manager went on to list time after time where Otis had demonstrated inflexibility that was problematic in working with others.

Otis found this tough to take, but he listened to more of what his manager had to say: "Even when new information comes along that shows us a better way, you hold to your original position. Once you've made up your mind, you won't even listen to what the others in the shop have to say."

Otis just couldn't develop the flexibility to work well within the organization and with other people. He could see the writing on the wall and left before the inevitable termination.

Action Steps

Ask three of your coworkers (and maybe your boss) to rate you on your flexibility.

If you score "average" or "above average," give yourself a pat on the back.

If you score very high, work on your ability to hold more firmly to a position; if very low, ease up and try being more flexible.

19
BRING ENTHUSIASM TO THE JOB

No one likes a grump. Putting enthusiasm into a task—or your work in general—will make it faster, easier, and more fun.

The Trap

Without enthusiasm, work is just work—tedious, boring, and grindingly slow. Somehow, we fall into the trap of thinking that since we don't really like our jobs or don't like being there, we need to demonstrate that to the people around us. So, we create our own hell.

The Professional Role

Enthusiasm infuses energy into every task and into our jobs as a whole. We get the work done faster, and it seems easier. Plus, enthusiasm creates its own momentum. Acting enthusiastic is the first step to really feeling enthusiastic.

In addition, when we are enthusiastic, other people around us often catch the same attitude. They become more enthusiastic, and that makes it more fun for us.

The key is to find a way to look at the task or job that allows us to focus on an aspect that we are interested in. Even if it's a task that isn't much fun, maybe we can become enthusiastic about getting it finished.

Enthusiasm creates some pride. We feel better and enjoy our work more. Plus, enthusiasm usually impresses the boss even more than anything else that we can do.

The Rule at Work

Brad was a travel agent working in a commercial travel agency. He had always dreamed of being a travel agent who booked wealthy people on exotic vacations. Instead he found himself booking businesspeople on trips to Toledo. He wasn't very happy about his job, but he had to pay the rent.

His attitude showed, and he knew it. He invited one of his coworkers to lunch one day. She seemed to enjoy her job, and Brad thought she might give him some tricks that would make the job go better.

She told him, "Brad, do you think I love booking the same trips from Kansas City to Detroit every day? No. But I want to enjoy my job and I want the time to fly by. So, I find things that can be enjoyable. I pump up my enthusiasm because I know that when I am more enthusiastic with people, they become more fun to work with. That makes my job more pleasant. It's sort of a self-fulfilling prophecy.

"Being enthusiastic breeds enthusiasm. I may start out the day just *acting* enthusiastic. Then others begin to play along…whether it's you guys at work or our customers. Then I catch the real thing. I become enthusiastic for real. Try it. Your day will go faster, and you'll enjoy your job a lot more."

Action Steps

Rate yourself on the Enthusiasm Scale from 1 to 10.

Identify three aspects of your job that you enjoy and use those to jump-start your enthusiasm.

Make this note and put it on your desk: I will be 10 percent more enthusiastic today!

Working with Others

20
SMILE

Smiling produces rewards. In addition to making work a nicer place to be, your relationships with everyone will grow...and that's key to having influence.

The Trap

Why don't we smile? We fall into the trap of believing that it looks silly or that it's dishonest. "After all, I really don't know the person so how can I smile at him?" Another version is "I don't really like anyone here, anyway" or "I don't feel like smiling."

The Professional Role

People may wonder why this is included as a rule for career success. Because it is essential for career success. We make progress in our careers through the relationships we create.

Smiling starts to create some level of relationship. People who smile are viewed as more friendly, more pleasant to be around, more upbeat, less threatening, more cooperative, and more team-oriented. People are more willing to help people they know and like. Smiling is an easy way to let people know that we're helpful, also.

Smiling makes us feel better. It's a great cure for a bad mood because it forces us to make some contact with another person. Sure, sometimes we have to fake it, but after a while, our inner feeling matches our smile.

Smiling has one more reward. When we smile at our coworkers and they smile back, the workplace is so much more pleasant and fun.

The Rule at Work

Myrna was one of 46 architects working for a famous architectural firm. She was recruited because she had a reputation for superior work. Because of that reputation, she was hired over the phone.

When she arrived for her first day at work, she was naturally nervous. She didn't smile once. The word quickly spread that Myrna had arrived and she was unfriendly and had a superior attitude.

Fortunately for her, her boss heard the rumors and talked to her at the end of the day, "Myrna, are you unhappy with your decision to join us?" She replied, "Of course not. I'm very happy to be here." The boss persisted, "Do you have any concerns now that you've met everyone and been here today?" Myrna answered, "Not really. It will just take some getting used to. I'm used to being around people who are a bit more friendly. No one smiles here."

The boss broke out into a big laugh, "Myrna, no one smiled at you because you didn't smile at anyone." She was startled, "Oh my gosh, you're right. I was so concerned about being accepted that I didn't pay any attention to how I was coming across. I can't believe that I didn't smile at all today. Do you think they'll hate me?"

The boss laughed again, "Of course not. But tomorrow smile at *one* person at least." With that they both broke into laughter, knowing that she would be smiling at everyone. Myrna's smile appeared for the manager as it did for her coworkers the next day...and every day thereafter.

Action Steps

Pay attention and smile at people today.
Pay attention and smile at people tomorrow.
Repeat steps A and B.

21
CHOOSE YOUR COMPANIONS CAREFULLY

You are judged by the company you keep at work. Right or wrong, it's still something you have to live with.

The Trap

Even if we recognize the practical truth of this rule, we still hesitate to change anything because we are uncomfortable socializing outside our sphere of friends. For some, being around higher-ranking people is difficult. For others, having only lower-ranking friends makes them feel superior. Finally, we may doubt that we have good enough social skills to socialize with other groups.

The Professional Role

Our companions—our social peers—represent how we see ourselves fitting in. Our social arena shows how we see ourselves as individuals and indicates our comfort level in being with different people. From a career perspective, we'll be slotted where we seem to fit. This works both positively and negatively, depending on the companions.

This is not to argue the rightness or wrongness, the morality or ethics, of this rule, but to present it simply as a practical career issue. It's one of those unwritten rules that people won't talk about and sometimes won't even acknowledge. Yet, it is absolutely true. It's not about dishonesty or inauthenticity; it's about perception.

It does not mean we should callously abandon our friends. It does mean that we need to face political realities and make choices.

The Rule at Work

Luis had an internship during his senior year of college. He came to the company eager to learn. His real hope, however, was to be offered a full-time job with the firm. He was assigned a mentor, Paul, who was a good guide and who liked Luis. Since Luis was in the top 10 percent of his class, was personable, and was hardworking, his future looked bright.

Luis and Paul focused on the technical work. Luis was outstanding. Paul was quite encouraged and brought Luis's name before the human resources committee for promotion. Paul was shocked when several members of the committee denied his request.

Paul asked for an explanation. They said, "Luis is a nice man and a fine technician, but he hangs around with Roberts and Ginall. They are difficult employees, always stirring up trouble. Granted, they are young like Luis and he probably feels some comradeship, but he shows no interest in associating with the analysts. You introduced them, and they were open to Luis, but he kept making excuses and avoided going to lunch or doing anything with them. We just don't think he's comfortable with the interaction at that level."

Paul told Luis the truth and it angered Luis. Understandably. Yet, he got the message. He didn't get the offer at this company, but he did at the next one, where he chose his companions carefully.

Action Steps

What message does your choice of companions send to your boss?

Target three people in your organization with whom you should cultivate a friendship over the next year.

Ask your boss to introduce you to an important player in your organization. Then cultivate that relationship carefully.

22
DON'T CONFUSE YOUR WORK LIFE
WITH YOUR FAMILY LIFE

Your boss is not your parent and your coworkers are not your siblings. Remember that, and you'll avoid lots of unpleasant situations.

The Trap

When we assume that the world operates the way our family did, we end up treating the boss like a parent, or at least having the feeling of being a child around authority figures. We also expect our coworkers to act like our siblings and treat us the way our siblings treated us.

The Professional Role

It's natural to believe that the world operates the same way that our family did. Our early family interaction formed the foundation for how we view the world. It was our first "group" experience. We naturally assumed that the world worked this way. However, that is not true.

Since we each come from different family situations, we each come with our own unique perspective. It's easy to see how chaotic the workplace can be (and often is) because of this. The key for us is to realize that our boss is not our parent and our coworkers are not our siblings. We need to meet the boss and coworkers for who they are, not for what they may represent to us.

We need to meet each person and each situation from a fresh viewpoint. This then gives us the freedom to create mature working relationships with the boss and coworkers. It makes work a healthier and more fun place to be.

The Rule at Work

Linda was an administrative assistant working for a demanding boss. She was frightened of him because he was assertive. In addition to that, Linda took the role of peacemaker at work. Whenever people were in conflict, she would rush to smooth it out between them. She'd talk to each of them privately and work out some sort of truce. Unfortunately, the truce only lasted until the next fight, when she would go through the whole process again.

She was experiencing a lot of stress because of this and thinking about quitting. Fortunately, she went to the company's employee assistance program and talked with an understanding counselor. The counselor asked, "Linda, how does your interaction with your boss remind you of your father?" Linda answered, "He's just like my father was. I was always intimidated by my dad, and now I'm in that situation again!"

The counselor continued, "And how does the interaction with your coworkers remind you of your brothers and sisters?" Linda was quick with her response, "It's just like home! I had to keep the peace. Otherwise they would have killed each other. I had to quiet them down before Dad found out, otherwise he would have been mad."

Linda just sat and thought for a moment. Then she said, "I get your point. I recreated my early family life here. I suppose that it would be the same if I ran to another job, wouldn't it?" The counselor said, "Your task is to see your coworkers in a new way, in a manner that allows you to remain an adult."

Action Steps

Ask two friends how their work is like their family life.
Tell them how your work is like your family life.
Pick a coworker and see how he or she reminds you of someone in your family.

23
COMMUNICATE EFFECTIVELY WHEN SPEAKING AND WRITING

Communication is the key to relationship. Relationship is the key to success. Communicate in the very best way you can.

The Trap

The primary trap here is to underestimate how important this really is to your career and success. Assuming that we communicate well or believing that we are unable to communicate are equally deep holes that we may never escape. There is always room for improvement.

The Professional Role

We all want to be heard and understood. We want to influence the people, events, and environment around us. That requires good communication skills. Plus, the way in which we communicate often determines other people's perceptions of us. It's the foundation of being successful.

There are two parts to communication. First, we must focus on what we want to say—our message. Then, we focus on how we deliver the message and how it is received—the emotional side of communication.

There are many ways to enhance communication skills. Observe successful communicators. Take a class or seminar. Read a book on speaking or writing. Get a coach. Practice, practice, practice.

The payoff: being taken seriously. Our professional image improves. Teamwork is enhanced. There is better cooperation and relationships.

The Rule at Work

Liam was a benefits counselor in the human resources department for a city in the south. He was smart and had a heart of gold, but he was often frustrated when people didn't take him seriously and when they politely ignored him and his ideas.

School was not Liam's favorite part of life, although he had done some college work. As such, he knew he didn't write very well. He tried to cover that up by being fun to be around. He would talk with people and be more playful than appropriate for his position. He would talk more than listen, so the employees often did not feel heard. He was fond of using "street language," which offended some people.

It may have taken a while, but he caught on that his communication skills needed some polishing. He asked his manager for feedback. His boss was pleased that he asked. He said, "Liam, you're a nice and fun guy, however, you need to consider other people's emotions when you talk with them. When they come to ask about benefits, they take that very seriously. You should reflect that in your communication style."

He continued, "You would do well to drop the swearing and slang. It isn't appropriate for the office. Over the long term, as you develop more, you should pay more attention to what you want to say, how you're saying it, and how it's being received. Then simply adjust when you sense it isn't working. Finally, let's get you into a business writing class. It isn't like fourth-grade writing, Liam. You might even enjoy it."

Action Steps

Pinpoint your communication weakness, and design a plan to overcome that.

Ask your boss and coworkers for feedback on your communications.

Where do you not feel heard when you communicate? What does that say?

24
LEARN FROM OTHERS

Keep that childlike curiosity about all that is going on around you. There is a vast world of teachers out there if we are willing to pay attention.

The Trap

There are three traps here. One is believing that we should only learn from authorities and highly educated people. The second is believing that we are not intelligent enough, so we give up on learning. The third is believing that we have all the knowledge we need in order to be successful; we assume that no one can teach us anything.

The Professional Role

We'll never know it all; no one does. The key is to be open to learning. A great way to learn is from others. We can observe them, ask them questions, learn from their mistakes, listen to their stories, or read about people who have similar experiences or who have experience that we could find valuable. We can watch, participate, and try what others show us.

Learning is not limited to formal education in a classroom. Sometimes the best way to learn is from the boss, coworkers, or customers. It's learning from people who have "been there." They have the practical experience. They have experienced it (for us). We don't have to do it all ourselves (the hard way). We can learn from others (the easy way).

The Rule at Work

Gary was an editor at a high-tech magazine. He was very intelligent and well educated, but a bit arrogant. He thought he knew it all, even though he had only started with the magazine six months earlier.

He found it difficult to pay much attention to other people's ideas or to accept that their way of doing something was better than his. As you can imagine, Gary's career didn't progress very well. In fact, he left the magazine and went to another publishing house. However, the same thing happened again.

When he was complaining to a good friend who knew what was happening, the friend finally decided to tell it like it was: "Gary, it might help if you were more open to learning from others. What have you learned from someone that's new recently? Try this as an exercise: Actively search for alternate ways of doing things, different ways of viewing the world, and new ideas and concepts that people have. Listen. Observe. Pay attention. Ask. You're going to find that others have a lot to teach you. Believe me, it's fun. It can be shocking. You may find their way is better. Occasionally, it will surprise and delight you."

Gary got the message. Of course, he still held his own positions and opinions in high regard, but also he gained a lot of insight, knowledge, and skills from others over the years. Now, he passes that on to others.

Action Steps

For practice, pay extra attention today to what you can learn from others. Make a list of 10 questions for which you'd like answers. Ask people this week.

Keep a learning journal. Each week write about something you learned from someone.

25

ASK THE BOSS WHAT HIS OR HER EXPECTATIONS ARE

Find out what your boss wants, needs, and expects. Knowing that will not only create a better relationship, but will also allow you to "win" in the job.

The Trap

People who make assumptions about what other people want frequently find that they are dead wrong. If we make this mistake at work we can find our careers stalled—or worse. As silly as it sounds, we make the mistake of assuming that we know what other people are thinking. Then we proceed to act on that assumption. In reality, we are only doing what we think is important or what we think they wanted.

The Professional Role

Smart employees find out what the boss wants, needs, and expects. This is not so much to impress the boss as it is to make sure that they are on track and that what they're doing makes the impact that it is supposed to make.

When we assume that we know what the boss wants, it is possible that we could miss the opportunity for some really good moves. When we find out what the boss wants, we might avoid some of the bad moves—those made not intentionally but out of ignorance.

There are two things that nearly every boss values: efficiency and effectiveness. Efficiency is doing things right. How do we know if we're doing things right? Ask. Effectiveness is doing the right things. How do we know what are the right things to do? Ask.

The Rule at Work

Carolyn transferred from the billing department to the purchasing office of her company. This meant that she had new responsibilities, a new working environment, and a new boss. Carolyn had been successful at her old job and wanted to be equally successful here.

Carolyn was very bright, and she quickly felt that things "weren't quite right." Some of the other team members sort of looked askance at the way she did some things. At other times, they actually seemed annoyed that she was doing certain tasks. Her boss was friendly and helpful but didn't seem overly enthused with her performance. She wondered what was wrong; while it didn't seem awful, it just didn't feel right.

She asked her boss for a meeting. She began, "I know what our purpose is here in the purchasing department and I want to be a valuable member of your team. I think I may have jumped in a little early and made a lot of assumptions about what you and the team want and need, as well as how to go about doing it. Can you review with me exactly what you want me to do and how you want me to do it?"

She felt a whole lot better after this conversation. Her priorities were now aligned with the department's, and everything felt much better. Her relationship with her coworkers and her boss developed to the point that she was soon considered one of the most valuable employees in the department. If she hadn't asked, she would have set herself up for failure.

Action Steps

Write the top five activities which you know that your boss values.

Make a list of 20 tasks you perform. Make a check by any that you think the boss might not want.

Make an appointment with the boss to check your lists.

26
CREATE RELATIONSHIPS

When we create relationships, we develop respect, trust, and cooperation. Relationships are based upon caring, and caring produces results.

The Trap

We may fall prey to believing how we interact with others has no impact on what we do. This is a false belief. Often this reflects what we're feeling from others around us. We believe that no one cares about us, so why should we care about them?

The Professional Role

We spend more time at work than anywhere else. It pays to create good relationships so that we're happier and not so lonely. It also helps us to get a lot more done, often in much easier ways. For example, it's much easier to get cooperation from someone with whom you have a good working relationship.

The joke is that it is impossible *not* to create a relationship with someone. The question is whether it's a positive one. Even ignoring someone involves some level of relationship. We have working relationships with our team members, boss, customers, suppliers, support staff, professionals in our industry, etc.

We create relationships by showing appreciation, openness, respect, trust, and attention, and by pitching in, sharing information, participating, caring, warning others of danger, cheering others on, and celebrating their successes.

The Rule at Work

Lani was a nutritionist at a famous health spa. She was brilliant and an expert in her field. However, she wasn't very comfortable being around people. Being a professional, she knew that creating relationships with people was simply part of the job. She did care about people. It was just not "her way" to show it much. Lani had to work at creating relationships because it didn't come naturally or comfortably to her. Yet, she was a real pro and she did it.

She went out of her way to acknowledge people—saying hello, commenting on something they had done well, thanking them for helping. She took time to meet people in other areas at the spa—the kitchen staff, the exercise instructors, the secretary in the administration office. She even took time to go down to the vegetable market where the spa got its famous "fresh daily" produce.

It always took energy for her to extend herself this way, but she acknowledged that it always paid off. She could work with the spa patrons better because she had a good working relationship with the chef. She could create better customer relationships because she could refer patrons to an exercise instructor who was particularly well suited for them. Several times there were visiting dignitaries, and she could get the vendors to order very special produce to please them when no one else could. She worked at creating relationships and enjoyed the results.

Action Steps

Go out of your way today to greet someone you don't know in the company. Give yourself a 1 to 10 ranking. How good are your working relationships?

Choose 12 people, or working areas, which would benefit from a better relationship with you. Work on one each month for a year.

27
PROVIDE GOOD CUSTOMER RELATIONS

Our job is really to serve our internal and external customers. Know what they expect, and add a little more. By doing so, we fulfill our promise.

The Trap

We often believe we do not have "customers," especially if we don't have people who hand us money. Or, we may believe that we can "get by with it"—meaning that we don't think people will notice or complain if we deliver poor service. We may even feel that they will come anyway because they don't have much, if any, choice.

The Professional Role

Customers are those who rely on us for assistance, service, or a product. They can be money-paying people in a store or the accounting department who works with our expense reports. It doesn't matter who. What does matter is that we want to provide them with our service.

We need to know what our customers expect. Knowing that, we have an obligation to supply it, within reason. We focus on availability, how the service or product is delivered, and the interpersonal interaction that is involved. In some ways, it makes a job harder. We must deal with interruptions. We must take time to interact with people. We have to be sensitive to people's feelings.

In reality, how we provide customer service is how people perceive us. Our reputations, our careers, and our companies' survival depend on providing good (or even great!) customer service.

The Rule at Work

Carol was a security officer at a downtown office building. She was sent to a seminar on improving customer service. She and her fellow officers giggled throughout most of it because it simply did not apply to their situation...or so they thought at the time.

"We don't have customers," they told each other. "After all, no one gives us money to buy an umbrella when it's raining. Sure, someone who sells something *must* provide good customer service. In fact, we demand that, because we're customers. But this doesn't apply to us."

Soon after that, they were all called in for a meeting with their boss. He began, "The building owners are considering hiring a private security firm to replace us. Yes, we protect the place well, but they say that we have not been responsive to the building tenants. We have had complaints from their customers and clients about the way they were treated when they asked us questions. Further, the owners say that we never help out in any way other than just security, so they're looking for a more 'customer friendly' group."

Needless to say a big discussion followed, with a lot of concern. After the emotion wore off, Carol and her colleagues came to the realization that they would become more "customer"-focused and try to keep the contract for themselves. They decided to reconsider the definition of a customer and to see the building's owners, tenants, and visitors as just that. They decided to not only do what was expected here, but also find ways to add a little extra.

Action Steps

Identify your customers.
Ask them what they want in terms of customer service.
Within reason and within your ability, provide it to them—plus a bit more.

28
SEEK FEEDBACK

We can't always see ourselves clearly. Seeking feedback involves seeing what we are doing, how we're doing it, and how that fits into the bigger picture— then, adjusting accordingly.

The Trap

We often believe that we already know how people see us. We truly think that we could predict what their feedback would be. Or we may not want to risk getting feedback, fearing that it may be unpleasant and painful. Finally, some people think that their contributions are not important enough to warrant feedback. All of these thoughts keep us in the trap.

The Professional Role

Feedback is the positive *and* negative information we receive from people on what and how we're doing things. When we seek it (or someone offers it!), we have an opportunity to give ourselves a pat on the back, to acknowledge what we're doing well. We also have the opportunity to see where we might be off track. Knowing this, we can make adjustments that will help us succeed.

When we get honest, objective, and helpful feedback, we can grow. We face reality. There is great power in this. It gives us a new and larger perspective. It makes our jobs more manageable because we know what to do. Don't be afraid to seek feedback. Often we are acknowledged, confirmed, and affirmed in our actions.

The Rule at Work

Sten was a dispatcher for a wheelchair-access van service. The company was rather small, with less than 50 employees. Sten felt confident about his work and about the relationships he had developed. However, he was the kind of person who was always open to improvement.

When he heard about the importance of getting feedback, he decided to try it. He asked his boss, several coworkers, and several of the drivers to give him feedback on what he did and how he did it. He had some specific questions and he also invited them to tell him anything that would be helpful for him to be great at his work.

His boss said, "Sten, I'm really glad you're on my team. You are on top of the daily routing, assignments, and efficiency measures. I would suggest you work on your communication skills with coworkers, as you tend to be rather short with them when you're stressed. Also, you tend to interrupt people before they finish." Sten was surprised about the communication issues, but he decided to notice if it was true.

He heard lots of comments from his coworkers, which included genuine praise and appreciation, along with some candid and insightful coaching for improvement. He recognized that this had taken time, but he was quite pleased. He knew where he stood. He was now free to make any adjustments in order to get even better feedback the next time.

Action Steps

Ask your boss for feedback on three areas of your work performance.

Ask your coworkers what they feel you do well; ask what two areas they think you could improve.

Go get a rich calorie-laden treat to enjoy as a reward for having the courage to look at yourself.

Conduct

29
BE ORGANIZED

Make a plan. Have a strategy. Being organized saves time, energy, and effort.

The Trap

Many people fall into the trap of believing that it's not necessary to be organized. They think, "Other people seem to get by without organizing themselves much. Why should I waste the time?" That's tricky because it does take a little extra time up front to get organized and that can appear to be a waste. This leads some people to begin thinking that they *save* time by not organizing. This is definitely the trap door for people who leap before they look.

The Professional Role

When we organize ourselves and our work, we save time, energy, and effort. Why? The "magic" of organizing lies in our thought process. That is, in the process of getting organized, we completely think through the job or task. We see how it fits together. We see what comes first, second, and third. Then, all the pieces make sense; the job makes sense; and we can work easily through the myriad of little things that the job entails…without getting sidetracked by going here and there.

We create more work than necessary when we fail to organize. Most of us would rather work smarter, not harder. Organization is the foundation of that.

This is the door for people who look before they leap. It makes the job more satisfying. It's easier. It also makes you look good at review time.

The Rule at Work

Rustam was the administrative nurse in a major hospital. He was in charge of all the paperwork for the floor. He had a reputation for being very organized and professional. Whenever new administrative nurses were hired for other floors, they were always sent to spend a few days with Rustam so that they could observe "how it should be done."

When newcomers arrived, Rustam would always start with the same little speech: "When I first came here, I was overwhelmed. There was so much to do. I'd start on one thing, only to be interrupted. Then I'd start on something else. I would start a job without thinking it through and would inevitably end up having to run here and there to get what I needed to finish it...and I wasted a whole lot of time."

He continued, "In my haste, I totally forgot to organize myself. When I fell behind, I wouldn't even do what little organizing I had done earlier. It all came crashing around me, until I spent my day off organizing my work. I mapped out all my routine tasks. I made checklists. I got all the stuff I needed. I planned my days and the end-of-month reports. Simply, I got organized. It was the best thing I ever did. Now my work flies. Because of that, it's more fun and I'm not overwhelmed anymore."

Action Steps

Make a list of tasks you need to complete today.

Outline a quick strategy to complete that list.

Take one recurring task that seems disorganized to you. Take charge and organize it.

30
BE FOCUSED

Focus forces you to concentrate. Concentration keeps you from getting lost in distractions. Result: the quickest route to achievement.

The Trap

There are so many distractions that many of us are tempted to lose our focus. Especially when aspects of the job are boring, we often want to get off track and go for what is interesting. Sometimes we want to do only the fun parts of our jobs and we may be lured into thinking that every moment has to be fun. We may find it more stimulating to do a "little here and a little there" in order to feel good. It doesn't work.

The Professional Role

Smart employees pay attention to the task at hand. By doing so, they take charge of situations instead of situations taking charge of them.

The key is to attend to one thing at a time and put all our energy behind it. We go through the tough parts and go through the boring parts. We avoid the distractions and channel our energy.

Keeping focus will allow us to complete the job much faster, and because we give it our full attention, we will probably have a much higher quality result. As a bonus, we will also be more aware of what's going on and will be able to respond faster and better to any problem.

Remembering what it is we need to do and focusing on doing it should be the guiding point of our working compass.

The Rule at Work

Joel was a customer service representative for a mail-order company. His career was going fine, but he just felt that he wasn't as productive as he could be. Joel really wanted a good evaluation and a possible promotion. He knew that in order to achieve that he would need to do something about his productivity.

He asked his boss for some candid feedback and advice. His boss smiled and said, "Joel, you have what it takes to be a great employee. You're intelligent, hardworking, and you care about this company. What's missing is your focus. You start something, then jump to something else, then go to even something else. You need to keep in mind the task at hand. Put all your energies into achieving it. Bring it to completion. Then go on to the next thing."

Joel responded, "But sometimes things need to be done that are more important than what I'm doing."

The boss countered, "True, on rare occasions something important does need to take precedence, but not all the time. Joel, how many different things are you working on today? How many things were you working on all at the same time yesterday?"

Joel knew that his boss was playfully cornering him. He got the point. He started paying attention to the task at hand, only being distracted if something was critical. His work improved. He got a great performance review.

Action Steps

Consider how many different things you work on at the same time. Too many? Get focused.

Rate your ability to focus on the job at hand now and set a goal for the future.

Try an "all-out focus" on your most important job today.

31
BE WILLING TO TAKE ON UNGLAMOROUS ASSIGNMENTS

The work of a great career is not all fun and glamour. The hard and unpleasant stuff is important, too. Do what needs to be done.

The Trap

The fantasy is that work should be fun 99 percent of the time and that we should always be doing "important," highly visible work. We have a tendency to want the glamorous assignments that provide us with prestige within the organization, with peers, and with management. The trap is believing a glamorous assignment is more important than an unglamorous one and that the tedious or unexciting work isn't important.

The Professional Role

A great career is made of good times and bad times, of glitzy and fun work and tiresome and boring work. Occasionally there are times when we get a chance to take on a glamorous assignment that offers high visibility and prestige. We should enjoy those times and work very hard to excel when given the chance.

However, professionals know that those opportunities are the frosting on the cake. They realize that they have to do a whole lot of work which is not visible, which can be tedious, and which isn't always exciting. Nevertheless, they do it with commitment and dedication.

Every organization counts on people to do the unglamorous tasks. If we do both the high-profile and low-profile work with equal dedication, the rewards will come our way.

The Rule at Work

Jackie wanted to be successful in her career as a customer service representative for a major airline. One day her boss asked for volunteers to work on straightening out the old complaint records in the storage rooms. Everyone looked around at each other hoping someone else would volunteer. This was not a fun assignment.

Jackie watched Liz who she thought was a role model in the department. Liz flatly refused, saying, "I'm not doing that grunt work. I'm a customer service professional. I shouldn't have to do things like that." Following her lead, Jackie also said that she wouldn't help. Finally, Sam, who would do anything, agreed to help out.

Jackie didn't have a good feeling about that interaction so she went in to talk with her supervisor the next day. "I've thought it over and I think I made a mistake yesterday…actually two mistakes," she said. "I feel badly because I didn't volunteer to do what would have helped this department, and secondly I subtly put down people who might have helped."

"I'm glad you had that insight and the courage to admit it," Jackie's supervisor responded. "When I consider who are my most valuable employees I always ask myself 'Who is it that I can always count on to do whatever is necessary to make this place work?' People who only take on glamorous assignments worry me. They are prima donnas. I need people who will do it all. We all have to pitch in. That's really what will get you noticed and appreciated."

Action Steps

How do you define work?

How do you respond to work that does not stroke your ego?

What is your personal job description? Does it match your boss's version?

32
PAY ATTENTION TO MISTAKES

Learn from your mistakes. Repeated mistakes can be fatal to your career. Pay attention and be conscious about what is going on.

The Trap

We often make mistakes because it feels "natural" to do it the way that we do, so we don't know (or notice) that we are making a mistake. The first mistake is not necessarily the problem. The problem lies in repeating a mistake.

The Professional Role

Making an honest mistake one time is not the problem. In fact, it can be an opportunity if we learn from it. The key is not to repeat it.

Mistakes are serious business. If we're sharp, we realize their importance—both from the problems they cause when we initially make them and from the potential for growth in understanding what we did wrong.

We must pay attention to what we are doing, especially after making an error the first time. Believe it or not, it's actually easy to repeat the mistake, because our minds have set up that pattern.

It's important to evaluate ourselves honestly if we are repeating a mistake over again. That's telling us something—about our attention or maybe something a bit deeper in our psyche. Perhaps we don't *want* to change and do it the right way. A bright employee knows that is a path to career problems.

The Rule at Work

Celeste was a telemarketer for a large office-products company. She had just transferred into this position from another department within the company.

Like most telemarketers, she was given a script to follow. She was instructed how to handle objections and how to close a sale. "If you just follow the script and follow the plan for interacting with customers, you'll do fine," she was told. The first week, things went very well. Celeste did fine, even though she forgot a line here and there, and made a small mistake on the order form. Once shown the proper way, she quickly adjusted and everything went smoothly.

However, things started getting off track the next week. Her supervisor corrected her, but she made several similar mistakes that week. In effect, she kept repeating the same mistake.

Celeste was smart. She sat herself down and asked, "Now what is going on here?" She decided that there were two things that were causing her mistakes. First, she felt she knew the script so well that she stopped paying attention. Second, she actually liked her ad-libs better than the script. However, she also knew that she needed to pay attention because her work was suffering. Although she liked her way better, she realized that the company was successful because it had developed a winning strategy. That little talk with herself was enough to get her back on track.

Action Steps

Pick one mistake which you seem to repeat. Determine why.

What did you learn from your last mistake?

Now that you've read this, help a friend learn from a mistake that he or she seems to keep making.

33
FOLLOW POLICIES AND PROCEDURES

Policies and procedures are there for a reason. Follow them. Not only will you protect yourself by doing so, but also you will benefit from the experience behind them.

The Trap

The trap is that we either don't take time to find out what policies and procedures are, or we don't follow them because we think that our way is best. We simply don't see the importance of understanding and following the rules.

The Professional Role

Despite what many people think, policies and procedures are in place for a reason. They are developed out of people's experiences in the past. Remember the old axiom that admonishes us to learn from our history lest we repeat it.

To most of us, that means following the rules because of the wisdom behind them and also the job protection that follows from doing so. As professional employees, we take it further. We find out why the rules were made—the reasoning behind them. That understanding allows us to do our jobs better.

There are times when following the rules can be difficult. Rather than ignoring the rule, however, the thing to do is to go to our bosses and ask them to help us understand the reasoning behind the rule so that we can overcome our resistance and get on with our jobs.

The Rule at Work

Ravi was a food processor at a specialty food manufacturer. He was eager to do well and enjoyed this job much better than his previous job at another company.

Most of the time Ravi had no problem following the rules. They made sense to him, and things worked out when he did follow the established procedures.

Sometimes, however, he wondered why things were done a certain way. Being a bright employee, he'd go and find out why. The reason nearly always made sense after it was explained to him.

One day, though, he came upon an unusual situation and went to the policy book to see how to handle it. It said, "To process an order with XYZ ingredients you must use special gloves." This made no sense to Ravi whatsoever. Besides, the gloves were awkward—so he didn't use them.

A month later, the entire batch of product came back, having prematurely spoiled. The reason? The oils from the other products, when exposed to these particular ingredients, made them become rancid quickly. Ravi learned his lesson.

Action Steps

Identify any rules that you don't understand and ask someone to help you understand them.

Choose the rule that you resist the most. Ask your boss to give you the rationale behind it.

Rate yourself on how resistant you are to rules. If you're very resistant, be honest with yourself about the real reason why.

34
THINK AHEAD

Part of your job is to think. Consider what will be happening later—this afternoon, tomorrow, next week, or next year. Reflect that awareness in what you're doing now.

The Trap

We get lost in the task at hand and forget to think about what will be happening later. We fail to consider the consequences of not thinking ahead. By not thinking ahead we lose the larger perspective, and consequently we may be going in the wrong direction or creating unnecessary work for ourselves.

The Professional Role

Forethought is a required ingredient for success. We do this by keeping in mind what is going to be happening. It can be as simple as thinking about what we are going to be doing tomorrow so that we can get what we need today in order to accomplish it.

It can also be much more complex and extend to our entire careers. We may need to look at what the trends are in our industry so that we can get the right training, education, or resources necessary to be successful in our jobs.

This is really about planning, organizing, and understanding our work and how it all fits together within the big picture.

The Rule at Work

Robert handled public relations for a regional temporary services firm. As he described it, "Since there is only one of us, I am the whole department." As such, he did not have the luxury of bouncing ideas off coworkers; and his boss, the vice president of marketing, was more interested in direct sales.

Robert knew that he had to think ahead in order to prosper in his job. Again, since he was a one-person department, no one was going to remind him of the upcoming special edition of the newspaper, or the charity event that the firm was sponsoring, or the changing nature of the public relations industry.

Robert formalized his approach to thinking ahead. Every day he asked himself what was going on tomorrow as well as the next week. That way he could do whatever was necessary to make it work. Then once a week he'd look ahead for the next few months and see what events were taking place, what promotions he had to plan, who he needed to talk with. That way, he was setting important work into action.

Finally, once every six months he would stop and reflect on what was going on in the temporary services industry as well as the profession of public relations. That way he was personally prepared for the future.

Action Steps

Stop for a moment and consider what happens at work that catches you off guard (that you haven't thought about).

Make a list of five things that will happen in the next month that you need to plan for.

Take some time and think of at least three major trends in the type of work you do and how you might want to respond to them.

35
YOUR ACTIONS REFLECT UPON YOUR EMPLOYER

To the customer, you are *the company. To people who know where you work,
you* are the company. *Positive or negative, your actions are judged as if they
are the company's actions.*

The Trap

Many of us believe that we are not identified with the company. We
believe that when we are off work what we do has nothing to do with
our job. Those thoughts can get us in trouble, professionally as well as
legally.

The Professional Role

The public assumes that our actions as employees are approved,
accepted, and promoted by the company. To customers, we are the
direct link. We represent the company. In fact, we *are* the company to
anyone who comes into contact only with us. If we serve a customer
well, the company is well represented and prospers. If we do poorly,
the customer believes the whole company is awful.

If we want to take a position or be active politically, socially, or professionally—and if we want that to be viewed as our position only and
not that of the company—then we take careful steps not to do anything that might link us and the company. We wouldn't wear clothes
with the company logo, use the company letterhead, or even introduce
ourselves along with where we work. Linking ourselves to the company suggests company endorsement. Think before taking such
actions.

The Rule at Work

Sandra was a nurse at an urban hospital. She went out of her way to be friendly and helpful with patients and their families and visitors. Over the years, she received many letters thanking her and saying what a wonderful hospital XYZ was. To the patients and families, she was the hospital and she represented it well.

Outside of work, Sandra had strong political opinions and was an activist in expressing them. One day a coworker who knew Sandra noticed that she was changing clothes before going off to a rally supporting one of her political causes. Her friend asked her why she was changing, "Why don't you just go in your uniform? It's only a meeting."

Sandra laughed, "Let me tell you. I won't make that mistake again! Several years ago I went to a march for a cause I supported. I wore my uniform with the hospital's name on it. Somehow I ended up on TV and they kept focusing on the hospital name. Our administrator, whom I happen to like and admire, had to field calls for days from people who opposed the march. I hold strong opinions, but it's not fair to this place to let people assume that the hospital holds the same opinions. So, it's simple. I change clothes."

Action Steps

Name three people to whom you are your organization.

Take note of people in other organizations and notice how well they represent their employers.

When you are next identified with the company (by a customer, member of the public, etc.) take a moment to think how that person may view the company because of your actions.

36
DO WHAT YOU SAY YOU'RE GOING TO DO

Do what you say you will do and people will trust you, believe you, and like you. Your "word" is who you are. This is how people judge you.

The Trap

It is so tempting to believe that it doesn't matter whether you actually do what you say you will do. "Nobody will notice." "This time it doesn't matter." "It's not important enough to make a difference." "I'm not important enough to make a difference."

The Professional Role

Think about the people you trust. You can count on them. They do what they say they will do. That's the essence of building a trustworthy reputation.

Establishing trust is important, not only for some moral value, but also for our relationships that develop with our customers, colleagues, and bosses.

People rightly expect that we will do what we say we'll do. If we come through, they will trust us more. As a result, we will be given more and more responsibility, authority, and rewards that go with being a highly trusted worker.

There's a bonus here, also. In addition to other people seeing us as more trustworthy, we'll find that we trust ourselves more. We'll have more confidence, be happier, and experience more success.

The Rule at Work

José was the scheduler for a delivery service. He had established a reputation as someone that everyone could count on. People respected him and liked him. He always did what he said he was going to do. On those rare instances when he simply couldn't deliver on his promises, he would get back to the person and work something out—and then do what he promised he'd do based on that agreement.

It really frustrated him when one of the new schedulers didn't live up to that standard. José tried to help him by hinting that he should simply do what he said he'd do, but the new guy wasn't much interested in hearing José's advice. He didn't do horrible things. He would just miss a deadline here and there, not follow up on a task every so often, or pretend to forget about an agreement on several occasions. People didn't think he was awful; they just didn't believe that they could count on him.

Over the next six months, the new guy couldn't figure out why everyone wanted to work with José and people avoided working with him. He felt that no one liked him, the boss was out to get him, and the other workers were "lowlifes." After about eight months, he left, never figuring out why things didn't work out.

José knew. People never developed any trust in the guy.

Action Steps

Pay attention today. Make note of any time that you didn't do what you said (or implied!) you were going to do.

Pick a day and make a list of all the "promises" you make to people. Check them off as you do them. Did you earn an A?

Renegotiate any agreements that you have failed to deliver upon.

37
BE A SELF-STARTER

Show initiative. Seek out things to be accomplished. Don't wait to be told what to do.

The Trap

It starts like this, "It's just a job. I'm really not responsible to do anything unless I'm told to." When we do walk this road we are perceived as lazy, unwilling to be a team player, and unconcerned about the success of the company.

Another thorny path is believing that we don't know what needs to be done. We get stuck in the "I don't know" syndrome. Most of us do know if we pay attention; and if we truly don't know, we could ask.

The Professional Role

When we take initiative and become self-starters, we are sending several messages: We are responsible; we care about the success of our unit, department, and company; we want to help our coworkers and bosses. These are powerful, positive messages that usually receive an equally positive response.

We display self-confidence when we're self-starting. In fact, we feel more in control of our work environment. Suddenly, we're a part of it, rather than just a cog in the wheel. We are making a real contribution.

Sure there are times when being a self-starter is difficult. It does take energy and initiative. And there are times when we do need direction, when we can't start ourselves. Those are rare instances, however.

In most cases we can be self-starters and display initiative. Then our colleagues and bosses will appreciate us. We will get positive attention; and rewards, such as pay raises and promotions, may follow.

The Rule at Work

Nenita was the project analyst for a large utility. She was responsible for research, planning, and oversight on various projects throughout the administrative offices.

When she started, she found herself overwhelmed with work. She didn't understand everything that was going on or that she was responsible for doing. She needed lots of direction. That was fine for a while, but eventually she became very knowledgeable and capable on her own.

Now, she was comfortable in her job but wanted to feel like she was more than just an average employee. She asked for advice from her mentor. Her mentor gave her a piece of advice that Nenita credits for her substantial career success since that time. The mentor said, "Nenita, it's simple. Be a self-starter. Go the extra mile. By showing that initiative, you will have everyone pulling for you. You'll stand out and you'll learn more. In addition, you'll feel better about yourself and your work. That will show, and you'll be rewarded for it."

Action Steps

Go to your boss and ask what you could do to help out.

When you get a few extra minutes, go to your coworkers and ask them what they need help with.

Determine something that needs to be done, which hasn't received attention and which you're able to accomplish. Then do it.

38
CONTINUE TO LEARN

Be willing to learn…for the rest of your life. It's essential. Learning keeps you alert, flexible, and growing.

The Trap

Some of us are frightened to learn something new. We say, "I already know enough." Even worse: "I already know it all." We don't. Some of us only defend what we know, rather than trying to learn something new. The saddest belief is that learning is boring.

The Professional Role

It's a cliché to say that the world is changing. Yet, it is. Learning is the way to change and *grow* along with it. Learning is much more than just attending classes or earning a degree. It can be reading trade journals or relevant articles about our job or industry in the newspaper or popular magazines. It can be attending a one-day seminar or a training class, having a conversation with an expert, or volunteering to work with someone who will teach us something.

If we don't learn new things, we get stuck in a rut. We need to get out of that rut and gain new perspectives. It's fun to keep our minds flexible and agile. Studies show that people who are curious and interested in learning throughout their lives actually live longer.

On a practical level, learning new skills and acquiring new knowledge keeps us competitive—competitive in job opportunities, promotions, and interesting projects. It also keeps us employable.

The Rule at Work

Felicita worked as a salesclerk at a large retail store for 12 years. She was getting bored with her job and she wanted to be considered for other jobs in the store. When she asked her manager what she needed to do in order to be considered for several of the job postings, the manager told her that she needed to learn the skills required for those jobs.

Felicita took a hard look at her present skills and then considered what new skills she needed to develop over the next year in order to be considered for the jobs she wanted. She determined that she needed to learn the basics of operating a computer, brush up on her math skills, and update her sales technique.

She had not enjoyed school when she was growing up, so the thought of attending a class didn't appeal to her. Instead, she bargained with another employee: Felicita would baby-sit her friend's children if the friend would teach her about computers. The friend readily agreed. Then, Felicita found a self-study workbook on basic business math. She liked learning at her own pace. Finally, she decided to attend a one-day sales seminar offered by one of the store's suppliers.

It worked. A year and a half later, there was an opening for a position that really interested her. She had the skills and she got the job.

Action Steps

Make a list of two or three skills that would be helpful to learn over the next few years.

Take stock of your skills today and match them with what you think will be needed three years from now.

Read something each week that will help you in your job.

39
KNOW WHAT YOUR RESPONSIBILITIES ARE

In order to succeed, you need to know what it takes to win. In other words, you need to know your responsibilities. If you don't know them, you can't meet those expectations.

The Trap

The trap is that, in the absence of knowing what we are actually responsible for, we make something up. Soon we come to believe that as the truth. Then we defend it as the truth. Finally, we get disappointed when we find out it is not the truth.

The Professional Role

The key to winning a game is to know the rules and how to win. It's the same for those of us working in organizations. We need to find out what it takes to win. We do so by asking our bosses and our colleagues. We don't just rely on the job description; we ask what are the real (and often unspoken) responsibilities that we have.

These change constantly, depending on what the organization needs at a particular time and what the industry and economy are forcing upon the company. A responsibility may be as simple as "You're responsible for covering the phones for Gail" or as broad as "You're responsible for giving me ideas to make this place work better so that we can all have jobs."

Not all responsibilities are equal. We may have a list of 20 things we're responsible for. However, there may be three, or five, or seven really critical ones—ones that we must always do...letting the others slide, if necessary. Again, the key is to *know* what you're responsible for. This is the way to succeed.

The Rule at Work

Linh was a research assistant at a brokerage house. He had read his job description and worked diligently at doing everything that was on it. Yet, he was disappointed when he received his year-end review. His overall rating was "satisfactory." He couldn't understand why he hadn't received an excellent rating, so he respectfully asked his manager.

"Linh, satisfactory is a good rating. It means you met all the requirements of your job," the manager told him.

"But I want excellent ratings. How do I achieve that?" Linh asked.

"First, you continue to meet all the requirements. Then, you work on some of the informal responsibilities that our associates have around here. For example, if you finish your work early, offer to pitch in for one of the other researchers. That's not in your job description, but it is a responsibility that I expect of all superior employees. Then, you can..." The manager outlined additional areas that would merit attention.

Linh was happy to learn *all* the responsibilities (both formal and informal) that were expected of him. He actually wished he had asked earlier. His next rating was "superior."

Action Steps

Without looking at the job description, see if you can list your job responsibilities.

Make a list of ten responsibilities that are not in your job description.

Ask three coworkers to tell you one responsibility that they suggest you work harder on. (Thank them if they have the courage to tell you.)

40
USE TIME WISELY

Time can be your friend or your enemy. Show respect for your time as well as everyone else's. Using time well shows responsibility.

The Trap

The trap is believing that everyone slacks off, does personal stuff on company time, and stretches breaks and lunch hours, and accepting that as part of the way things are done in organizations. Another pitfall is believing that no one will notice.

The Professional Role

Time is an organization's most valuable commodity. It's also important for employees. How we manage our time reflects our professionalism, and it forms the basis for how our bosses will perceive us. If we want to create a great reputation, we need to use our time wisely.

It can be the simple things like showing up for work on time, all the time. It's keeping to our scheduled lunch and break times. It's not wasting time talking with coworkers (too much) or doing personal business on company time. It's staying focused on a task and doing real work in the time allotted.

Another aspect to time management is that of maturity. When we manage our time well, we are signaling that we don't expect others to have to manage it for us. We are saying that we don't need our boss keeping us on track. Using time wisely is simply being responsible—and not wasting a valuable resource.

The Rule at Work

Arthur was a technical support specialist in computer operations with a manufacturing company. By nature, he was very organized and honest.

However, when it came to managing his time, he wasn't so good. He would come in late occasionally, take long breaks, and call his girlfriend at least three times a day. When he did his job, he worked like a madman; and when he finished, he'd go talk with other people who were in the middle of their jobs.

His supervisor cut him some slack because "techies" march to a different beat. However, Arthur's use of time got worse. So, he and his supervisor talked about what needed to improve.

It was a struggle for him at first. He didn't like the constraints. He even considered resisting her recommendations and rebelling. Fortunately, he was smarter than that and did make an effort to use his time more wisely. He found that it wasn't that difficult.

In this process, he discovered that he was more efficient and productive and he had more fun. He realized that his little rebellion against time management was just part of his developing into a "real adult" (as he put it) and as a professional in his field.

Action Steps

Determine the areas in which you use your time to its fullest advantage (or where it is your friend).

Now, do the opposite. Determine areas where you use time poorly (or where time has become your enemy).

Choose the aspect about time that gives you most trouble and vow to correct that over the next 30 days.

41
DEVELOP SELF-DISCIPLINE

Self-discipline is the foundation for success. In effect, it's being your own manager.

The Trap

The trap is the desire to stay a child, where we're controlled by external forces—first, our mother and father; and now, bosses. Instead of taking personal responsibility for our behavior, we let other people take responsibility for us. Then, we get treated like a child.

When we fall into this trap we usually don't believe in ourselves very much. We don't believe that we can be responsible for rewarding and punishing ourselves appropriately. Quite honestly, when we don't develop self-discipline, we're being lazy and inviting people to force controls on us from the outside.

The Professional Role

Self-discipline is being our own (internal) manager. It's riding herd on ourselves. In effect, it's giving ourselves our own performance reviews.

Self-discipline involves nearly all aspects of our working life. We live up to our commitments. We stick with something until it is finished. We face up to the tough assignments.

As strong people, we manage ourselves—setting good rules, boundaries, and expectations. We find ways to reward ourselves—a mental pat on the back or sharing the success with a friend. When we don't do so well, we honestly acknowledge our lack of self-discipline, fix any messes we've created, and commit to being more disciplined next time.

The Rule at Work

Silas was excited about his new job as a claims processor for a large insurance company. This was his first "real" job since graduating from college.

Prior to this, Silas sort of went along in life. His parents were happy to influence many of the major decisions in his life. His professors told him what to study and when. His girlfriend usually put up with his lateness and forgetfulness.

Silas tried this same laid-back approach on the job. It didn't work. He got a poor performance review. It stated, "Fails to take initiative; poor time management; doesn't always complete tasks." Silas started to resent his manager for monitoring him so closely. In reality, he hadn't developed professional self-discipline, so it was being imposed on him by other people.

Fortunately, the pain of going through this was greater than the pain of changing. So, Silas developed the self-discipline necessary to get other people off his back. In the process, he found that self-discipline was more fun and gave him a much better feeling about himself.

Action Steps

Take 10 minutes to review your level of self-discipline. What are you good at? What needs improving?

Identify at least one of those improvement areas and commit to being disciplined about it. Next month, add another.

Each week, give yourself a "pat on the back" for improvement.

42
BE CONSISTENT IN WHAT YOU DO

Consistency establishes credibility and trust. People learn to count on you. It defines your performance and who you are.

The Trap

The trap is believing that consistency doesn't matter. We hope that our bosses and fellow workers will only notice and remember those things that we do well. However, they also remember when we don't do things well.

The Professional Role

It's better to be consistently good than to have moments of brilliance followed by times of sloppiness. Consistency builds trust. It's important that our bosses and colleagues can count on us, can trust us in a working environment. We establish a pattern, and people then say to themselves, "This is how she works, so I can interact with her knowing the outcome."

Consistency is saying and doing our best at all times. Consistency is producing the same high quality results in our work over and over. Consistency is interacting with people in the same professional and pleasant manner whenever we work with them. Consistency is establishing a pattern of reliability and predictability. In other words, in our work and in our relationships we come across the same way all the time, so that other people have a good sense of who we are and how we work.

Being consistent sends the message that we are reliable and predictable. People count on us when they are confident in the work that we do. Being consistently good usually leads to greater responsibility.

The Rule at Work

Sharon was graduating from college and interviewing for the position of accounting clerk at a regional bank. She had high hopes for her future. She had earned A's, B's, and a few C's in college. She worked on and off during college and produced a very good senior project.

Fortunately, she had a recruiter who gave her some honest feedback. He said, "Sharon, you obviously know accounting and you're a pleasant person to talk with; however, I am a bit concerned about the lack of consistency in your educational pattern. I am looking for employees who will do consistently good work, will be consistent with their commitment, and will establish a pattern of working well with people."

He continued, "I don't expect people to get all A's, but it looks like you only got them in classes related to accounting. That makes me think that you might only do well when you like something. But the world of work involves doing things that you like as well as things that are pretty boring. Furthermore, you were only employed sporadically during college. Did you only work when you had to? When I see this pattern I worry that a person might not find any particular enjoyment in working and will perform only when the economic pressure is on."

Sharon got the message. She admitted that she had never seen it from this perspective. She committed to being a consistently good employee and the firm hired her.

Action Steps

What are three patterns you have that demonstrate consistency?

Identify at least one pattern where other people might see you as being inconsistent.

Think of a person who consistently performs well at work. How do people interact with that person?

Ethics

43
HAVE INTEGRITY

Integrity is adhering to a set of values. It's acting in a way that makes us feel good about ourselves. It starts on the inside and shows up on the outside.

The Trap

Some people believe that having integrity in the workplace is old-fashioned and out of style. Many assume that the way to get ahead is to forgo integrity. We separate our actions from our responsibility—for example, we stretch the truth with a customer, when we would never lie outside the work environment.

The Professional Role

When we have integrity, we feel good about ourselves. It's an internal feeling, an internal job. Yet, integrity manifests itself on the outside in our actions toward people.

Integrity is more than honesty. It is the congruence between the way we think, the way we act, the way we respond, and the way we judge ourselves and others. It's living in such a way that those are all balanced. In other words, we think, act, respond, and judge in ways that show our depth of character. We're then seen as trustworthy and solid. Without integrity, we're seen as shallow, sleazy, and untrustworthy.

It is easier to act with integrity when we consider in advance some of the moral dilemmas we may face. Each of us needs to know our bottom line (what we will and won't do) in advance. We each have our core beliefs about what is right and wrong. Trust those beliefs.

The Rule at Work

Belinda was a financial planner for a major investment company. Because she was licensed and a member of her professional society, she had agreed to live up to a published code of conduct. That was easy for her. She knew the rules and thought about them beforehand and accepted them. She lived her life and conducted business accordingly.

However, she came to realize that having integrity was much bigger than just following the professional rules.

She wrestled with these dilemmas: "I say that I will do something, but other things come up. Do I follow through or handle the emerging issue? I could recommend either investment for my client, but I'll make a lot more money if I recommend X. Do I recommend X? When my client asks me to reveal confidential information from my company and threatens to close his account unless I do, what do I do? I promised my family I would spend weekends with them, but now my company wants me to work on Saturdays...."

Belinda discovered that having integrity required some effort and involved some gray areas. She thought a lot about this and made some decisions about what she would do, wouldn't do, and where she was flexible. That helped her through the times when she felt she or someone else was questioning her integrity.

Action Steps

Give yourself a rating on how well your values match your actions.
Determine any areas where you have concerns. What do you need to work on?

Get an object or toy that will remind you to keep your integrity about this matter. Keep it on your desk.

44
DO NOT CHEAT, STEAL, OR EMBEZZLE

Stealing is not a fringe benefit. It's simply wrong. We're entitled to our pay, not more.

The Trap

We often feel as though we are underpaid, unappreciated, and deserving of more than we're getting. So we *take* something to make up for it. "I deserve it," we tell ourselves. "After all, I'm just getting even. It's a payback…besides, everyone does it." We think the company won't miss it or that no one will notice.

The Professional Role

There is no denying that some of us are underpaid, and there is no denying many of us feel unappreciated. Yet, we struck a bargain: a day's work for a day's pay. No more, no less. An ethical person honors that contract.

This is one of the highest points of ethics. Cheating and stealing are just wrong. This isn't intended to be preachy, just a reminder of what we all really know. Sure, people can find all sorts of rationalization and justification. That still doesn't change the true nature of this.

From a practical viewpoint, there are the obvious outcomes. Someone *will* be watching, eventually. When caught, we will be embarrassed, humiliated, and possibly terminated. Careers may be ruined and lives destroyed. It's just not worth it.

Ultimately, we have to live with ourselves. Who wants to live with an unethical thief?

The Rule at Work

Carl was the property manager for a large apartment complex. He was a good man, middle-aged, fairly average in most ways. Because he had a college degree, he had expected to be further along in his career. His job was a good one, but he had expected more. Plus, the company which owned this complex was known for paying relatively low salaries.

Carl had some reason for disappointment. He knew that several other property managers "supplemented" their income by pocketing a cash payment here and there, and by "borrowing" some supplies, equipment, and material. Certainly, this tempted Carl.

Carl's mind was starting to go down the wrong path; but his heart was solid. He allowed himself to get angry, to express his disappointment to his family and friends, and to turn that anger into action by looking for a better company and a better boss. But, he didn't steal. He didn't embezzle from the rental account. He didn't cheat the renters or the suppliers. He maintained his ethics.

This didn't make Carl a rich man, nor did it remove his anger or disappointment. What it did give him was self-worth, self-esteem, and a solid reputation. He did not put himself or his family at risk. He didn't lose sleep because he felt guilty. He lived with the pride that he was a good and honest man.

Action Steps

Reflect on your own ethical dilemmas. Decide what the I-will-not-cross line is for you.

If you're doing something wrong, stop it.

Surround yourself with honest people. Don't hang around with people who cheat and steal.

45
USE DRUGS AND LOSE

How important are drugs and alcohol in your life? Can you live without them? Don't substitute altered states for true relaxation and enjoyment of life.

The Trap

We slip into this trap when we start believing that we need drugs or alcohol to relax, feel good, or escape our problems. Then we convince ourselves that it's harmless, "After all, everyone's doing it. Anyway, I could go without it if I wanted to."

The Professional Role

Drugs and alcohol impair our judgment. Thus, they impair our career decisions and actions. This is not about having a beer after work with friends, and it has nothing to do with a morality about drinking or using drugs. It is about using drugs and alcohol as substitutes for authentic communication, real relaxation, and healthy resolution of problems.

Altered states are inconsistent with high performance. When drinking or taking drugs, we sacrifice judgment and clarity. In losing our inhibitions, we may say or do things that damage our career.

Peak performance requires that we get enough rest. Another aspect of peak performance is the ability to relax. Be kind to our bodies and minds. Physically and psychologically, we all need downtime. Find healthy ways to relax and unwind. It's worth the time and effort.

The Rule at Work

Bob had recently begun his career as a computer systems administrator. He had always loved computers and was very eager to progress in his field. He worked hard and he worked long hours—sometimes 60 or more hours per week.

Bob instinctively knew that he had to relax, and he also wanted to have as much fun as possible on his rare moments away from work. He started with just a few beers on the weekend, which was no problem. However, it grew to heavy drinking and using drugs with his friends.

He'd go back to work on Monday feeling a little groggy and more tired because he had partied as hard as he worked. He didn't notice it, but he was losing his edge. He still functioned at work, but he was missing the clarity he'd had earlier. He was slower and his decisions weren't as insightful.

His manager asked him, "Bob, is something going on? You're different from when you first started. I can't quite put my finger on it, but you seem distracted. I've told you before to get enough rest. If you need more time off, by all means arrange that."

Bob didn't listen, and his career started a downhill slide. That is, until he met Liz. They started dating. Bob really wanted this relationship to work. Lucky for him, Liz wouldn't put up with his drinking and drug use. She insisted that he take time off and rest. She suggested talking with a counselor. She insisted on quality time together and real communication. Bob found himself again, and his career regained its former momentum.

Action Steps

Make a mental log. How much do you rely on drugs or alcohol?
Develop three interests that allow you to have fun and relax naturally.
How would your life be different without drugs or alcohol?

46
ADMIT IT WHEN YOU DON'T KNOW SOMETHING

No one knows everything, so remember that it's OK when you don't know something. Ask. Find out. Then move on. Don't try to hide it. Otherwise, it will come back to haunt you.

The Trap

We all want to look good, smart, successful, and infallible. Consider the "costs" of hiding our lack of knowledge. We focus on the wrong side of the equation. Underneath we fear that people will ridicule us for not knowing something or, even worse, that we might be fired. In fact, we're much more likely to be fired for *not* finding out something than for asking.

The Professional Role

No one knows it all. Bosses don't expect their employees to know everything. They *do* expect them to find out what they don't know if it impacts the business.

Exceptional employees know a lot. Not everything, but a lot. They also have great personal skill at knowing what they do know and what they don't know. When they don't have the answer or they don't understand something, they find out.

No one wants to look stupid, and that's not what this is recommending. Quite the contrary, it's suggesting that smart people ask questions. They explore. They research. They are curious. That's what sets them apart.

The Rule at Work

Haley was an accounting clerk who had just changed companies in order to prepare herself for a possible promotion. She felt that her new company would offer her more challenge and, thus, she could grow more professionally.

When she started she met with her boss and they discussed her new duties. "You've done the accounts payable before, haven't you?" he asked. "Of course," Haley replied. In fact, she had, but when she saw the method this company used she was totally confused.

She worried a lot that night when she went home. She thought, "They will think they have hired the wrong person. They will think that I don't know what I'm doing. They will think that I lied to them when I told them I knew how to do accounts payable."

Finally, she could stand it no longer. She felt that her integrity and professionalism were on the line. She decided to take the risk and admit that she didn't understand their system.

When she told her boss the next day, she was both shocked and relieved. The boss said, "Oh, I'm sorry I forgot to go over the peculiarities of our system here. Thank goodness you asked for help, otherwise you could really have had problems. It didn't make any sense to me either when I first came here."

Action Steps

What is one thing that you don't know or understand at work, which you've been hesitant to acknowledge?

What would happen (really) if you admitted that you didn't know something?

Go ask a question that will help you do your job better.

47

DO NOT ENGAGE IN SEXUAL OR ROMANTIC
RELATIONSHIPS AT WORK

At first, having a romantic relationship with a coworker seems uncomplicated. It's what happens later that's the problem. Think carefully before leaping. An office romance might be tempting, but it's playing with fire.

The Trap

Too often we've seen people fall into the trap of believing, "We can handle it. Besides, our relationship is different. There will never be any problems at work as a result of this. We can separate our work from our personal lives. Besides, we'll never break up." Or it might be, "Nobody will ever know. We're very discreet."

The Professional Role

Engaging in sexual or romantic relationships at work is risky at best, lethal at worst. We *do* get to know each other well at work. It's where we spend most of our time. Many people report that they feel closer to people at work than to many of their friends outside work. It's easy to see how one could be tempted to become involved.

It's just a bad idea. It's fraught with potential problems. Of course, there are the potential legal consequences with sexual harassment charges. Even consensual relationships that go bad can result in charges as a "punishment" to the "offending party."

There is an awkwardness that occurs when people are around those who are romantically involved; roles may become confused. Results: embarrassment, loss of trust and respect from boss and coworkers, humiliation, or job loss.

The Rule at Work

Rick was an accountant in the corporate headquarters of a manufacturing company. He was single, worked a lot, and didn't socialize much. Not surprisingly, he developed some close friendships with his coworkers.

Along the way, he was working on a special project that involved several members of a task force. The project required some late-night and weekend work. As the project went on, Rick and a female member of the task force became closer and closer, clearly leading to a romance. They didn't think anyone noticed until a good friend of Rick's teased him about it one day in the company gym. Rick was shocked. He realized that if this guy knew, everyone did.

It was really tough for him, but Rick asked the woman to dinner to discuss the situation. He told her, "We've both admitted how attracted we are to each other. Nothing has changed for me in that regard. However, I see problems developing at work because of this. Since neither of us wants to transfer out of the department, we will need to work together for a long time. People are already talking. I notice some of them acting strange when they're around us. I even notice that I act awkward around you during the workday. In the long run I'm afraid it may affect our careers."

They were depressed because it was this way, but they knew it was true. They knew it was best to focus on friendship instead of romance. They did, and in the process they maintained a great friendship.

Action Steps

Develop social contacts outside work.

If you're thinking about becoming involved, talk with a trusted friend about the potential consequences.

If you're still tempted: still don't do it.

48
KEEP CONFIDENTIAL INFORMATION CONFIDENTIAL

Don't share any information that might harm anyone else, harm your company, or harm yourself. Also, don't share private information which is vital to the success of your company.

The Trap

We insist that there really are no secrets so we feel justified in telling—thinking that it doesn't matter. Or we rationalize our behavior by saying that we just can't keep a secret. Also, we may fall into the trap of using information as a source of personal power, to be popular, or to trade for something we want to know.

The Professional Role

We're not hired to do newscasts. Sure, it may be tempting to share something really juicy that is confidential, but it simply is wrong.

Confidential information could be anything from personnel records to the strategic marketing plan for a new product. A guiding rule is this: Is it possible that *anyone* or *anything* could be harmed by sharing this information? If yes, then just don't do it.

Clearly, if we share confidential information we risk our careers and, in some cases, face legal consequences. On a more personal note, it violates our own ethics and integrity. Sharing that knowledge gives our power away. We need to maintain our integrity and trustworthiness at all times, no matter what. By doing so, we maintain the trust of those around us and of the company as a whole.

The Rule at Work

Henri was a medical transcriptionist. He had access to all the patients' medical records in the clinic. He was also very good with his word processing skills, so he was often asked to prepare official documents for the doctors and the clinic.

Henri had no problem keeping the clinic's information confidential. He knew the strategic plan, the acquisition strategy, the building plans, and all the contract information with suppliers. He knew that it was important for the very survival and success of the clinic that this information be kept private. He maintained that confidentiality, and felt proud of his professionalism.

Henri faced a big dilemma with his friends, however, over his desire to share personal information about some of the clinic's more famous patients and also about the information he knew that was in the clinic's personnel files. He knew that he could be the most popular and interesting person at a party with just a few tidbits about these issues. Henri was really tempted...and he knew that if he resisted, he would be pressured by his friends not to be such a "company man."

He did, however, resist the temptation. He kept confidential information confidential. It certainly wasn't easy and he had to fight himself on several occasions. Yet, he maintained his integrity and ethics and he earned and kept his bosses' respect and trust.

Action Steps

If you're sharing confidential information, stop.

If you've been able to resist the temptation, do something nice for yourself tonight to acknowledge your professionalism.

Vow not to pressure others to violate their confidences.

Self-Development

49
BE A ROLE MODEL

Set the pace and tone for your work group. Take pride in your work. Don't be afraid to stand out.

The Trap

This trap is a strange one. We're afraid to stand out and show our true talent and abilities. We fear that people won't like us if we become a role model. Thus, we hide our real ability and settle for less.

The Professional Role

We all need to take pride in our work. It gives meaning and purpose to our lives. A role model is simply someone who has full command of the job, meets the challenges head-on, has good relationships with coworkers and management, and exhibits the positive values of a good person and a good employee.

As employees, we have enormous power to set the tone of the work environment. Even if we're temporarily stuck with a bad boss, we can still take pride in our work, get along with and enjoy each other, and meet or exceed expectations. All it takes is a willingness to do our very best. One person *can* make a difference. If we rise to the challenge, we'll be seen as more promotable and more capable. People will notice and follow our example.

The Rule at Work

Richard was a mortgage lender in a national bank. When he joined the bank, he noticed that everyone seemed to do "just enough to get by."

Not knowing any better, he fell into step with them, matching their level of work.

Over a year or so, he observed other bright and eager people who joined the operation. They came in anxious to do really fine work and to excel, but they rather quickly adapted to the pace and tone of the group.

Richard liked his coworkers, and they liked him. He wanted that to continue, but he was also frustrated with mediocrity. He knew he could do better. He felt that he was stifling his spirit. He vowed to himself that he was going to step out and become a role model. He knew it might mean some dislike from his pals, but he was willing to risk it.

He began working at the level that he had originally planned. He still maintained good relationships. A few people seemed to be annoyed, the majority didn't pay much attention at first, and a few rose to the challenge and enjoyed the new standard being set.

Eventually, higher expectations emerged, and most employees strove to meet them. New employees had role models to follow, adding even more to the group's achievement level. Morale increased and most people said they felt better about themselves and their work. All of this, because Richard was willing to be a role model.

Action Steps

Pick an aspect of your work and start to become a role model in that aspect.

Make a list of 10 expectations your company has for an outstanding employee.

Find a role model and learn from him or her.

50
KNOW HOW YOU WORK BEST

Learn your working habits and style. Know what you do well naturally and how you do it. Take advantage of those strengths.

The Trap

Some habits are helpful and others don't serve us as well. The trap occurs when we try to completely change our style or adapt it to situations where it doesn't work. If you have a habit of being detail-oriented but get so lost in the detail that you don't finish things on time, you're caught in the trap.

The Professional Role

There is great power in knowing yourself, and particularly in knowing how you work, what you do best, and what habits get in the way.

The first thing to do is to realize which habits and elements of your style are really strengths. Consider when you do things well. Think about how you work best with people. Know how you think.

Secondly, deal with those habits that get in the way. Determine habits in your natural work patterns that no longer serve you well. Eliminate those organizational work patterns that inhibit you. Perhaps most importantly, recognize and change those habits and patterns that prevent you from working well with people.

Professional employees know themselves and use that knowledge to their benefit and to the benefit of the organization.

The Rule at Work

Carlo was a bright and energetic lead accounting clerk. He was valued by management, and his coworkers liked and respected him. One day a new employee joined Carlo's team. Carlo could see that Paula, the new clerk, was having some problems. He offered to help. At first she was reluctant, thinking that it showed she was a bad employee, but Carlo assured her that he had been through the same thing when he started.

"So, what's your advice?" she asked.

"Well, like all of us you have some things you do naturally well, and others that aren't particularly helpful. For example, I've watched you these past few weeks and here's what I noticed," he began.

"You seem to be great at the detail work, and you get along well with your coworkers. Your communication skills are one of your best strengths. I'd suggest that you take advantage of your strength in handling details by asking about the purpose and method of the work before you start."

This made great sense to Paula, who took Carlo's advice (even seeking out more advice as they worked together over the years). Paula now gives similar advice to her new coworkers.

Action Steps

Determine one natural strength and one weakness in your organization skills.

Determine one natural strength and one weakness in your people skills.

Make a simple list of overall work habits you want to enhance and those you'd like to diminish.

51
KNOW HOW YOUR BOSS THINKS

Don't assume that the boss thinks the same way that you think. Learn what the boss values. Pay attention to the boss's working style.

The Trap

The most dangerous assumption we can make is to think that the boss thinks exactly like we do. Or, we may assume that it doesn't matter how the boss thinks because the job outcome is the only thing that matters.

Another dangerous assumption is to believe that it's obvious how the boss thinks. Warning: Just because you and the boss came to the same conclusion once upon a time, doesn't mean that you think alike.

The Professional Role

It's imperative to know how the boss thinks as well as to know and understand the boss's working style. Our performance is judged through the boss's values and through the lens of his or her working style. There are rewards for knowing the boss's expectations and matching them, and there are dangers in not meeting the boss's expectations. The key is to know what the boss considers important at work and elsewhere.

How do we learn about the boss? We need to observe behavior, notice what is rewarded and what is punished, and pay attention to what is talked about. Also, we can tune into the more subtle behavior clues: body language, tone of voice, eye contact, timing, and the feedback given to individuals and the team.

The Rule at Work

Bill was a loan processor at a large bank. He had begun his career as an intern and had a boss he enjoyed. He felt that they thought much the same way and, as a result, he experienced a lot of success.

Then Bill became a full-time employee and was transferred to another loan processing unit. Suddenly, he had a new boss. Bill kept doing things the way his old boss would have wanted. When he received feedback from his new boss, he was shocked to discover that she felt he was "out of touch" with what was needed in the department.

After he got over being upset, he intuitively knew that he had to figure out his new boss. He needed to learn how she thought, what she valued, her expectations, and her working style.

He asked for feedback directly. He was surprised to discover that some things he *thought* she wanted, she didn't. On the other hand, there were certain behaviors that she really valued that his old boss didn't.

Bill was also surprised to learn that just because she agreed with him on one issue didn't mean that she'd agree with him on a different one. Of course, that made perfect sense to him after he noticed it, but before that he had assumed that they would agree on everything.

Eventually, Bill learned how his boss thought and realized how important that was to his success.

Action Steps

Identify your boss's top five expectations for you.

With a trusted coworker, discuss how the boss thinks. See if you both agree. If not, it's time to pay attention.

Pick an important project. Ask the boss to teach you how to think through a project like this.

52
BE CAREFUL HOW YOU QUESTION THE RULES

Learn to disagree without being disagreeable. Focus on the rule, policy, or issue—not the person behind it. Avoid personalizing it. The person must not feel attacked.

The Trap

We're in dangerous territory when we make the assumption that rules are "just rules" and that they are not connected to anyone. At worst, we might be tempted to question things because we *do* want to be disruptive or attack someone personally. Another danger is believing that all rules are questionable. There are some core rules that companies hold so dearly that questioning them gives the appearance of disloyalty.

The Professional Role

It's in *how* we question that we either help our careers or hurt them. Remember: in order to get respect, we must give respect. We need to be sensitive to how our questioning is being perceived. We must understand that there is a chain of command. There is a way to challenge. The lower we are in the company hierarchy, the more we want to ask cautious questions before challenging a rule; the higher we are, the more comfortable we can be with the direct questioning of a rule.

The general rule is to keep the focus on how the issue is pertinent to our work situation and how we are able to produce or not produce because of it. It is also good politics to acknowledge the good intent of the rule and rule maker before questioning it.

The Rule at Work

Rob was a social worker who was young and very idealistic. When he was hired, his bosses and coworkers really liked that enthusiasm.

Perhaps because he was so idealistic, he began to question a lot of the rules, policies, and procedures. While he had good intentions, he presented his questions rather forcefully. To many people, it almost felt like an attack. They would respond, of course, giving Rob the reasons behind the rules and the logic for keeping them in place. More often than not, Rob saw the wisdom behind the rules.

Then Rob fell into the habit of questioning everything. Many people felt that he was nit-picking—questioning things that really didn't make any difference anyway.

After some time, his bosses and coworkers grew tired of his constant and aggressive questioning. They told him so. Rob was shocked, because he never intended to come off as a troublemaker. He said, "I only want the best for this department. I never knew that's how it felt to you."

To Rob's great credit, he *did* have the department's best interests at heart and promptly proceeded to ask questions only about important issues, letting the unimportant ones alone. He also became very sensitive to how he was being perceived when he asked a question. He was talented and quickly learned how to question and disagree without being disagreeable.

Action Steps

Ask two friends how you are perceived when you're asking questions.

Ask them how they perceive you when you are disagreeing with them.

The next time you question a rule, pay special attention to how you're questioning it and how the question is received.

53
CREATE A SUPPORT SYSTEM

Have friends you can rely on, both inside and outside work. In order to feel whole, we must have safety, respect, care, and love in our lives. Trusted friends provide that.

The Trap

We often use the excuse that we don't have the energy to develop deep friendships because we work too much. In fact, our failure to develop deep friendships may stem from the fact that many of us don't trust other people...certainly not enough to let them see our vulnerable side. Another problem may be that we don't know how to create a support system.

The Professional Role

We all need to talk with someone about what's going on with us. We can't hold it all inside. It's such a gift to have trusted friends we can share our triumphs and our tragedies with. This is true around work issues as well as personal ones.

It's an interesting fact to note that people who do not create support systems are much more likely to get into trouble, react negatively to setbacks and mistakes, act inappropriately, and even become ill.

A support system (friends, family, trusted advisers) not only gives us a shoulder to cry on, it also gives us an outside perspective around work issues. It is our reality check with the world.

It's tough to have good friends, because we have to be a good friend in return.

The Rule at Work

Kathryn was a biologist working in a government program. She was friendly at work and with the people in her apartment building, but she never really developed deep friendships.

At one point, problems started occurring at work. Kathryn wasn't the cause, but she felt caught up in the drama of the workplace. Her stress level rose. She was both angry and a little frightened because she didn't know how things would be resolved. She found it difficult to concentrate on her work and to meet her assigned objectives.

She found herself talking to her cat about her concerns at work. As she sat home one evening, feeling very lonely and isolated, a college friend called. Kathryn let all of her frustrations and feelings out to her friend, who was very supportive and gave her some very helpful ideas on how to deal with the situation. Kathryn said, "I'm so glad you called. I needed to talk with someone."

That incident shook Kathryn up. She realized that she had no one that she could be herself with, no one to share her good times and bad times. She decided to talk with her minister and ask for some advice. He said, "Kathryn, I know it's tough to develop quality friendships. It's going to be a little scary, but you have to initiate the contact and you have to *be* the kind of friend you want to have. If you do that, over a period of time, you'll have a great support system. Then, if you should ever need to talk with someone at 2:00 a.m., someone will be there for you."

Action Steps

Write the names of friends who you could ask for help at 2:00 a.m.
Talk with a trusted friend about what is going on emotionally for you.
What does it take be the kind of friend that you want others to be for you?

54
DEVELOP PEOPLE SKILLS

In reality, there is no such thing as an organization—there is only people. To survive and prosper, you must learn to work effectively with people.

The Trap

The biggest trap is believing that we can be successful without people. "I'm so talented; it doesn't matter how I interact." "I generally work alone, so I don't really have to get along with people." "People need to get along with *me*." Then there are smaller traps: believing that other people are the problem; believing that technical skills and talent are enough; and believing that we're not people-oriented.

The Professional Role

It's absolutely critical that we find ways to develop positive working relationships. We're not on islands by ourselves. We need to create relationships, communicate, provide great customer service, etc. Our careers depend upon being able to get along with and work with people—from the day we interview and are hired to the day we leave.

We all have models for getting along with people. As children we found ways to successfully get along in our families and in school. As adults we can watch other people who have great people skills. See what works. Model that behavior. Listen. Ask for help or guidance. "Try on" other people's way of interacting within the world. Have curiosity about others and how to interact. When we do all of this, we naturally develop better people skills.

The Rule at Work

Nancy was a computer programmer. She was smart, technically competent, and eager to have a successful career. However, she was never interested in developing her people skills. Early in her career she discovered that she needed cooperation from other people, despite the fact that she primarily worked alone. She asked for guidance from her boss, who was very glad to provide a few insights and offered several very helpful suggestions. Nancy's professional people skills were starting to develop.

When she was having her performance review, she asked her boss what it would take for her to get a promotion. She told him that she was willing to work hard to reach that goal. "Nancy, your technical skills are fine, and I've noticed a real effort on your part to get along with other programmers as well as other people in the company. That's a great start. However, to progress further, you'll need to develop even stronger people skills."

He continued, "For example, you'll want to learn how to influence others without using power or threats. It would be helpful to develop some social contacts within the company so you have allies and support—as well as people to keep you in touch with the rest of the organization. You might also benefit from taking a class in conflict management, since you seem to have a difficult time with conflict. So, just work on those people skills and you'll certainly be considered for advancement."

Action Steps

Read Dale Carnegie's How to Win Friends and Influence People.
Who is a good role model at work for people skills? Watch that person and learn.
Ask your boss for candid feedback on your people skills.

55
FIND WAYS TO ENJOY YOUR JOB

If you can't find a way to enjoy some part of your job, you can't stay there. It will kill you emotionally and physically.

The Trap

Some of us think, "Work is work. Don't expect to enjoy it." We may even believe that we don't deserve to enjoy it. Another trap is thinking that there isn't any part of the job which could be enjoyable. Another version of this is, "I'm afraid to enjoy any part of this job because I'll end up staying here forever."

The Professional Role

We should focus on the positive aspects of a job, not the negative. Once we identify the positives, we can expand them and spend a little more time on the tasks that we enjoy. That will make the unpleasant ones bearable. When we do this, we can at least take pride and satisfaction in some parts of our job—if not all of it.

Without some enjoyment on the job, work becomes meaningless. And we as human beings aren't very good at doing meaningless tasks. On some level our jobs must nurture us. Just getting a paycheck isn't enough. Without some enjoyment, we become depressed, lose energy, feel detached, and fade away. We show up physically, but not emotionally.

The way to feeling alive in our jobs is to find some aspect of our work in which we can have an emotional investment. We need to care about something, whether it's taking pride in making the best sandwich or creating the best architectural design. The key is to find what makes *us* feel good and focus on that.

The Rule at Work

Kristine was a dietitian at a retirement village. She had been at this job for 17 years. She felt bored and somewhat depressed. She no longer liked coming to work. On the other hand, she was positive that she did not want to change jobs or go to another place.

One evening she found herself becoming angry about her boredom. She started talking to herself, "Kristine, you've got to snap out of this. You just can't continue to go in with this attitude. It's killing you." Afterwards, she started laughing because her advice to herself was so perfect.

Kristine decided that she was going to find some way to enjoy her job, so that she could feel good about herself. First, she made a list of things that were pleasant about her job: two coworkers who were fun to be around; her freedom in creating the meals; and the special dinners and events she would plan. Then she made a list of things that were OK, neither positive or negative: meeting with the administrator, presenting her report at the end of the month, and reading her professional literature.

After making the lists, she set out to find ways to enjoy the tasks on the lists. (Note: She didn't even bother making a list of the things she didn't like. She figured that she had focused on those enough.)

Action Steps

Change aspects of two job tasks so that you could enjoy them.

Pick several more aspects of your job that you like somewhat. Explore ways to make them even more enjoyable.

Find people you enjoy at work. Spend more time with them.

The Future

56
YOUR WORK IMPACTS YOUR LIFE

Choose your work environment consciously and carefully. Why? Just as events in our personal lives impact our work, our work experience impacts our reality.

The Trap

We delude ourselves into believing that a job doesn't have that much impact on our lives. Some of us have even tried to shut off and ignore the negative emotions that certain work environments reflect.

We think, "It's just a job. I can leave it all at work." Or, "It does not have any impact on who I am."

The Professional Role

We need to be conscious that our work environment will impact who we are and how we see the world—both positively and negatively.

Of course, there is no "perfect" place to work...but there are *better* environments. The goal is to find an environment that nurtures us personally as well as professionally. If we can't do that, then we need to find ways to make our work situation as positive as we can and to minimize any negative aspects.

All of us have to work, and jobs are not always easy to find. We do what we have to do. Yet, we need to understand that we are largely the sum of our experiences. Thus, if you have an opportunity to choose where you work, or who you work for, consider which environment would make you happiest.

The Rule at Work

Allen was the dental technician for three dentists. When he graduated from school, Allen had a tough time finding work. He interviewed with the dentists at this practice and was offered the position. At the time, he really needed a job, so he ignored his own instincts which told him that this was a pressure-filled office with hard-driving partners. Allen would have preferred a gentler environment, which fit with his personal style.

He soon found himself stressed by the pace and the demands that were placed on him. He did well, but he found himself getting moody and having little energy for quality time with his life partner. The work was really impacting his life. Yet, he needed the paycheck.

Being a sharp guy, he decided to make the best of it. He took breaks. He exercised to get rid of some stress. He was even able to make some modifications that improved the work environment.

As a result, Allen's mood picked up and his personal life improved. He was prepared to stay there into the foreseeable future. However, when a position opened with another dental practice that had a more relaxed atmosphere, Allen decided to take it. He didn't go because the current job was so horrible. It wasn't. He had found ways to make it work. Rather, he went because he knew that his life would get even better if he worked in a place where he felt really good in the environment.

Action Steps

How has your outlook on the world changed since working for your current company or in your industry?

If you're looking for work, make a list of the kinds of places and the types of people you want to work for and with.

If your work is damaging your life, make a plan to get out. Then, do it.

57
MOVE ON BEFORE IT'S TOO LATE

Never stop looking for new opportunities. Being comfortable now may be the most dangerous time in your career. Never sacrifice your career for comfort.

The Trap

"I've worked hard to get to this place in my career. I just want to enjoy it." That's how we are tempted to think. We may even believe that we won't ever *have* to move on (new challenge, new job, new department, new company, etc.). Some people are terrified at the thought of changing and moving on, be it a small or a dramatic move.

The Professional Role

Seize this time to explore and develop. We need to follow that advice before it's too late. We need to deepen our understanding of our jobs— to be flexible and learn—so we become the most valuable employee possible. Often, that means keeping our eyes on the big picture of our industry and our profession as a whole. We all know that jobs, companies, and the economy are changing. We need to develop ourselves and have the courage to move on in our careers before we get trapped.

We want to move on *before* we are forced to, whether that's because of cutbacks, changing skill requirements, competitive or industry changes, or our own mental health. We want to move on before we damage our emotional or physical health. We want to move on before the boss tells us about a layoff. We want to move on before we feel compelled to "burn bridges" in anger.

The Rule at Work

Sylvia was a data entry clerk. Every morning she had this sinking feeling that her job was going to be eliminated. The company had already cut the number of data entry clerks by half. She had heard stories of other companies eliminating this type of position entirely. She was scared, but still, she took no action.

The day she feared finally came. She was laid off. She was angry and very frightened. "What am I going to do?" she asked herself. Now, she was forced to leave...and she didn't like it.

Fortunately, she found a similar job at another company. This time, however, she was determined to make her next move on her terms! She enrolled in courses that updated her job skills. She joined a working women's group to network about job openings and to keep a pulse on what was going on in business. She watched for job postings within the company to see if there were jobs she wanted to explore.

In fact, she found another job within the company, working in the new computer information center. Her studies had paid off. But did that stop her? No. She kept learning more and more, networking, keeping abreast of the profession and industry. She heard of another interesting and challenging job at another company. It meant a promotion, more money, and greater challenge. She took it. She was proud of her progress from three years earlier when she was laid off.

Action Steps

If you suspect that it's time to move on, it is! Do it.

Learn one new skill each year that will help your career.

Establish at least five business contacts outside your company. Learn what's going on in other places.

58
LEAVE THE OLD JOB BEHIND

When you start a new job, take the skills, knowledge, and experience with you. Leave the old position, people, and company behind.

The Trap

We begin a new job by comparing it to the old job. We fail to start with a clean slate. In fact, we often begin to romanticize the old job, the old friends, and the old company. Because of the natural discomfort of beginning anew and out of a desire to impress people, we start saying how good it was at our old job, how they did it better, and how much more meaningful the relationships were.

The Professional Role

People are not much interested in what was. They're interested in today. What we did in the past is history. Any time we start a new job, we're being asked to look and move forward—not back. Quite honestly, other than getting us the job, our success "there" means little to nothing "here." We must produce here to be successful.

We must establish a new foundation wherever we go, whether it's to a new company or a different unit within the same company. While bringing experience, we must honor the culture of the new workplace.

We're given a blessed opportunity when we go to a new job. We can start anew, unhampered by our past mistakes. We can start clean. We have the opportunity to build an even greater future. We can establish great new relationships.

The Rule at Work

Tony was a general support-staff employee working in the Department of Aging for state government. He sought a similar position in another department of the state. When he was hired, he was very excited. He thought it was his chance to move ahead in his career.

Soon after he went to the new job, he started telling his coworkers "how we did it over in my old department." He did this so often that his new coworkers were starting to complain about it behind his back. One day after he had done this again, he was very surprised by the outburst of a fellow employee: "Tony, we don't care. You're here now. What do you think—that we're all stupid here? You keep telling us how smart people were there and how wonderful it was. How do you think that makes us feel?"

Tony realized his mistakes. He hadn't concentrated on learning the new department before he tried to change it. He saw how that could really annoy people. He hadn't spent time developing new relationships. He saw how that made him seem aloof. He had wanted to impress his new coworkers and boss so much that he went overboard.

There was only one thing to do. Admit it—quickly! He spent the next day talking with people. He told them, "I made a mistake trying to hold onto my old job...and I was too foolish to notice how I was coming across. I want to be a part of this team and I want to work well with you."

Action Steps

Do you ever make suggestions saying, "At XYZ we did it this way"?

Spend at least 90 percent of your business-social time with people who work where you're working now.

Stop comparing your old job with your new position. You're here now.

59

THIS JOB IS PART OF YOUR CAREER

You're on your career path whether you want to be or not. From the moment you started working, it began. The question is what you want to do with it.

The Trap

The most pervasive trap is "I don't really have a career yet. This is just a job." After that, the next warning sign is wanting our career to miraculously appear. We hope that "it" will appear naturally. We deny that our careers have started because we don't know what we want to do. Or, just the opposite, we think that our current job will last forever and that our current job *is* our career.

The Professional Role

Our career is the sum of our employment history—past, present, and future. Whatever we are doing to support ourselves *is* part of our career. Many people think of a career as their favorite job or the one which they're in at this time. Not so. Our career is our whole working experience.

We need to avoid seeing our current job as our whole career. If we get trapped into doing that, we may miss the opportunities that present themselves because they don't fit our current mental picture of what our career is. Be open to the possibilities. We can also look for ways that our current job will help us in the future. Every skill we learn can help us in some way in the future part of our career.

The Rule at Work

Jessica was a bookkeeper for a nonprofit social services agency. She had bounced around from one job to the next before she joined the agency. She started off bagging groceries at the local Safeway. Then she went to secretarial school and worked as a do-everything secretary in a small office. Next she opened a small catering business, which failed.

After she closed the catering business, Jessica was quite depressed. She felt that all of her friends had careers and she didn't. Fortunately, Jessica found a career counselor who was able to help her.

The counselor told Jessica, "You've had a career since you began bagging groceries. All the jobs you have held and will hold will equal the sum of your career. The question is not whether you will find a career. That's done. The question is how your career will unfold and how you will influence its direction."

This was new to Jessica. But with the counselor's words in mind, she decided she had two primary goals and a secondary one. She wanted to be an accountant and she wanted to work in an organization that focused on doing good things for people. Her secondary goal was to explore being a manager.

Jessica swung into action. She knew she'd have to take accounting courses and began the shaping of her career. Her previous experience helped her to obtain the future positions she wanted.

Action Steps

Make a list of the jobs you've had so far in your career.

Beside each, list five (or more!) skills you developed from each.

Make a list of 10 career moves that would intrigue you. If one stands out for you, begin to set things in motion.

60
DON'T BURN YOUR BRIDGES

Create relationships. Don't destroy them. That's true even when you're angry or unhappy. Bad endings have a way of haunting you.

The Trap

The trap is that there is no perfect organization or boss and "burning your bridges" really hurts you more than it hurts others. It is easy to believe that how you leave a job will have nothing to do with your future, or to become so angry that you don't care how one situation will affect the next.

The Professional Role

Professional employees know that their long-term careers depend on relationships, including professional relationships with former bosses and companies.

Even if they don't think they need those relationships, professional employees realize that bad mouthing a boss or company reflects on *them*. New prospective employers will probably look down on someone who is so negative about past people and experiences. They will likely wonder if the prospective employee will say the same things about them or this company.

That's why it's so important to maintain good working relationships. We may find ourselves needing a good reference or even working for the same company or boss again if there is a reorganization or merger. We might even discover that the old boss or company wasn't so bad after all, and we may want to go back. Friends come and go, but enemies last forever.

The Rule at Work

Sharon was so excited about her first job. She was the order supply clerk in a mail-order clothing company. She found that she disagreed with the boss about how things should be done, but she wanted the job so she cooperated. Soon she decided to search for a new job.

She found one working for a retail company as a salesperson in the women's clothing department. When she left, she decided to blast her boss and the company. "I don't think you know what you're doing, and this is a horrible place to work, " she said in her exit interview.

While working for the retailer, she found that she liked it better but still had a few differences with the boss and the company. Despite that, she decided to apply for a management intern position. It required that she have letters of reference from her last three supervisors. She knew the old supervisor would not provide a good reference.

To Sharon's great credit, she decided to face the issue head on. She went and talked with the personnel representative and told her the truth. The personnel rep was understanding but gave her some clear advice. "Sharon, occasionally you will run into a bad boss or have a bad working experience. Certainly you should try to improve it. If you can't, it's OK to look for another job. So you're fine as far as that goes. However, even when that happens, don't burn your bridges. Go ahead and leave, but leave professionally. Maintain relationships, don't destroy them."

Action Steps

Identify any bridges (working relationships) that you're tempted to burn. Look back; are their any bridges that you can and need to repair?

Vow to honor yourself and your career by maintaining good relationships rather than damaging them.

61
MOVE FORWARD

You must develop the attitude that you can *change. You must grow in order to survive and prosper. Don't get locked into believing that things will always be the same as they are today.*

The Trap

We fall into the trap of believing that nothing will change, that our situation or work environment will be this way forever. Then we're stuck in the rut. We may believe that it's too hard to keep up or to change...or that we're too old. We may say, "I've been at this job too long; I can't do anything else. My skills are just too out of date."

The Professional Role

All aspects of our lives change, including our jobs. Don't be intimidated by that. In that change, every situation has potential. Seize it. This is true even if we don't want to expand our careers or be promoted. We still must move forward to maintain our jobs.

How do we do that? The first step is attitudinal. We must be open to more perspectives than the one we currently hold. We must see the changes and the options that go with them. Further, we must *believe* that we are capable of changing.

We must think entrepreneurially. Our *skills* are what we are paid for, not for showing up to work. Thus, we must update and enhance our skills every chance we get. We need to see what skills are valued and decide how we can get those. We must move forward.

The Rule at Work

Noreen was a pharmacist for a national drugstore chain. She had been a pharmacist for 18 years. She was an outstanding employee. This was due in large part to her willingness to move forward within her job. Early in her career, she saw that she was going to have to change and grow in her profession.

She told us, "When I started most pharmacies were free-standing mom-and-pop stores, which also had soda fountains. People paid for their own medicine. Then insurance started covering some of the expenses. This meant that I had to understand insurance, copayments, and billing, in addition to understanding medicines. Then came a wave of drugstores closing because the large discount stores put pharmacies into their retail outlets. We had to compete on price and learn about marketing as well."

She continued, "Then there were the changes in laws and in the legal aspects. We always had to be careful, but when lawsuits started getting out of hand, I had to learn the legal aspects of my job as well as new recording procedures. Later, I saw large retail stores focusing primarily on pharmacies. There are now megadrugstores in every major city. Because of that, I had to learn about HMO contracts, merchandise sale tie-ins, and medicine by mail. It's been a wild ride, but it's been fun. Thank goodness I was able to move forward with all the changes...and I suspect there will be even more in my future."

Action Steps

What skills would you be required to have today to be hired for your job?

List all the reasons you have for not moving forward. Find a way to break down those barriers.

Decide on the most important skill you need to develop. Work on it now!

62
SEEK TRAINING AND EDUCATION

This is not optional. You never know too much. Training and education keep you flexible, strong, and growing. Unless you grow, you wither away.

The Trap

It's mainly our thoughts about training and education that trap us. "Learning is for the young, not for me...I'm too old." "I can't afford it." "I don't have the time." "I didn't like school." Or, we may have become lazy and decided that there is nothing that we're interested in.

The Professional Role

If we're not growing, we're dying. Once upon a time people thought that education was for children. Students believed that once they had "graduated" it was over and they could get on with their lives. It wasn't true then, and it's even less true today.

Learning is a lifelong process. All of us need to continually update our skills and add new ones. We need to update ourselves and gain new perspectives. That's why we need to seek education and training. When we do, we find that we have more mental flexibility. We're more promotable. We're more mobile, should we decide to pursue other jobs.

Civilization is changing at an unprecedented rate. If we don't change with it, we're going to be unmarketable and we'll eventually settle for the lowest rungs of our job ladder...if we can maintain the job at all. The hard truth is: sometimes we have to do things we don't like to do simply because we have to do them. Whether or not we enjoy learning, in the end, education and training are not optional.

The Rule at Work

Curtis was a retail merchandiser. He was responsible for the product displays in an upscale department store. He was good at his job, which he had held for the last five years.

His manager had encouraged Curtis to attend several of the store training sessions, but he had always found some excuse. "I don't have time now." Or, "That particular topic doesn't directly apply to me." His manager also encouraged him to attend a week-long seminar on the latest merchandising techniques. Curtis had another excuse. "It's just a party atmosphere at those seminars. Besides I know it all already."

Curtis got a gentle shock and unpleasant surprise when he attended a district meeting where all the retail merchandisers from the various stores met to plan events for the following year. It was clear that several of the other merchandisers had learned some great new techniques. One even gave a presentation on the changing aspect of retail operations.

It dawned on Curtis that he really did need to get more education and training. To his great credit, he did so with vigor. He attended the store training, even when it wasn't directly relevant, because he could still learn something about the business and apply it in his line of work. He asked his boss to recommend any other seminars which might help, and he reenrolled in college to finish his degree.

Action Steps

Enroll in one course, training class, or seminar within the next six months. Buy a book that will enhance your knowledge. Read it.

Make a list of the reasons that have stopped you from seeking education and training. Beside each, write a plan to overcome it.

63
TELL EVERYONE WHAT YOU NEED

We are all interdependent. We don't operate successfully in isolation. Take a little risk: Be visible and ask for what you need.

The Trap

The trap is fear. When we ask for what we want and need, our fear surfaces—the fear of being dependent or of owing someone something in return. We also might be afraid of letting others know something about us—especially that we don't know everything.

The Professional Role

Sharing our needs and wants can make us stronger. We may learn better ways to do something. We may get information to make our jobs go better. We may secure resources that we need in order to be successful. We can receive outside influence to knock down barriers or open doors. In short, we can get what we need to be stronger and more successful.

Give and take. It's the way of business. It's the way of the world. Most of us would be happy to help other people out if we could *and* if they asked (or at least let us know that they were looking). It works the same when we ask. We can start by asking our friends. They may even help us refine what we're looking for, as we often are not clear the first time around. Then we can proceed to casual acquaintances, bosses, coworkers, etc. The more people who know that we are searching for something, the more people who are potentially available to help.

The Rule at Work

Ray was the only photographer in the audio-visual department of his company's corporate headquarters. He had worked there for several years and, although he enjoyed his work, he realized that there was no career growth at this company. He knew that if he wanted to move up, expand his responsibility, or increase his pay, he would need to move on.

He looked in the want ads, read the help-wanted sections of professional magazines, and sent many résumés. But nothing happened.

One day he complained to a friend, saying that even though he was doing all the right things, he wasn't finding a job. The friend wisely asked, "How many people have you told about your job search?" "No one," he replied. His friend said, "You need to tell everybody what you need because you never know who will be able to help you get it."

Ray listened, and to his delight he found that people did help him. As it turned out, the head janitor at his company was living with a woman who worked in the personnel department of a larger company that was searching for a new photographer. Ray interviewed there and got the job. If he had not taken the time to share his need, he would never have gotten the unadvertised job.

He found that asking for what he needed and wanted was easy, fun, and *very* helpful. He also found that people like helping others if you give them the chance.

Action Steps

Choose something you need or want. Tell at least 10 people this week.

Repeat step A next week.

Listen to what people are telling you that they need. You may know something that is helpful. It works both ways.

64
PLAN YOUR RETIREMENT NOW

Take inventory of what you really want in your career and in your retirement. Develop a plan to get it. Start now (no matter how old you are).

The Trap

Most of us deny that we're growing older...or that we will ever *be* old. We're afraid of it. Thus, we ignore it and get caught later on. Over the past few decades, the American culture fostered a belief that "someone will take care of me (the government, the company, or Social Security)." We all recognize this trap.

The Professional Role

Retirement is a transition, not an ending point. If we have enough money (which takes planning and discipline, but which is possible) and we have goals, retirement can be a very rewarding time of our lives.

It's never too early to plan for retirement. It's so much easier if we start young. All we have to do then is set aside a little money each month someplace where we won't touch it until retirement, and continue to explore our goals and interests throughout life, and we're set when retirement comes.

Sounds easy. It is, if we do it early. However, most of us never believed that we were going to get older, and retirement seemed an eternity away. It happens. When we reach retirement, we wish we had started planning earlier. Begin planning now!

The Rule at Work

Jacque was a human resources representative for an international construction management company. Everyone liked her. They saw her as a role model. Employees would say, "Jacque's on top of everything. She thinks ahead...even about her retirement, which is still eight years away!"

It was true. Jacque realized that retirement was just a transition point in her life, not an ending. She set a goal for herself upon retirement. She planned to spend six months touring South America. To prepare, she enrolled in a community college course on world geography. Two years prior to retirement, she was going to study a language for her travels.

One day Jacque asked a young employee, "Have you started planning for your retirement?" He was shocked at the question and answered, "No. I'm only 28 years old." He seemed to think that settled the matter. Not so with Jacque.

Jacque looked directly at him and said, "Young man, it's *never* too early to start. You go and sign up for the payroll deductions in the company retirement program today. Saving a little each month will be painless now. Then, when you approach retirement age like me, money won't be a problem. You'll simply have to decide what you want to do."

There can be a huge payoff for a little planning and discipline.

Action Steps

If you haven't started a monthly contribution to a retirement plan, start today.

If you have started one, take at least one-third of your next raise and increase your contribution.

If you're within 10 years of actual retirement, make a 10-year plan preparing yourself for your next big life adventure.

About the Authors

BRUCE N. HYLAND is a West Coast consultant in organizational development who has worked with clients ranging from K-Mart and Payless Shoes to the city governments of Palm Springs and Oakland, California. A former executive with American Express and Director of Management Studies at City College of San Francisco, Dr. Hyland conducts seminars nationally and internationally.

MERLE J. YOST, a former consultant, is a licensed psychotherapist. He has advised both for-profit and not-for-profit organizations, including Southland Corporation, the March of Dimes, and the Muscular Dystrophy Association. He is currently in private practice in Oakland, California.